THE SCREAMING EAGLES
The 101st Airborne Division in World War II

A thrilling, fast-paced story of the 101st Airborne Division. The author recounts all the blood and sweat, successes and failures of these brave men. The three most significant operations the 101st took part in are described. There is the invasion of Normandy, where the 101st had to pave the way for the landing on Utah Beach. The exciting events are re-enacted as the division attempts to secure the area for the Allied invasion. Then there is Operation Market-Garden in Holland. Holland's geography posed a major threat to any rapid advance by the British. The many canals and rivers crossing the country made it easy to implement delaying tactics by the retreating Germans. The division's job was to seize a sixteen-mile stretch of road that began behind the German front line. This roadway was to be called "Hell's Highway" by the troopers of the 101st. The final section of the book recalls the momentous, history-making Battle of the Bulge, Hitler's last mad gamble to win the war. The Screaming Eagles would help write that history and play a vital part in it, with an exhibition of superb, unflinching courage in a Belgian city they would make forever famous: Bastogne.

The Division's last daily bulletin, written by their colonel, stated in part, ". . . be proud that you are of the 'old guard' of the greatest divisions ever to fight for our country. Carry with you the memory of its greatness wherever you go, being always assured of respect when you say, 'I served with the 101st.'" This book is a fine tribute to those courageous, dedicated men.

BOOKS BY MILTON J. SHAPIRO

ALL STARS OF THE OUTFIELD

BASEBALL'S GREATEST PITCHERS

CHAMPIONS OF THE BAT: Baseball's Greatest Sluggers

HEROES BEHIND THE MASK: America's Greatest Catchers

JACKIE ROBINSON OF THE BROOKLYN DODGERS

THE PRO QUARTERBACKS

THE SCREAMING EAGLES: The 101st Airborne Division in
World War II

A TREASURY OF SPORTS HUMOR

THE YEAR THEY WON THE MOST VALUABLE PLAYER AWARD

THE
SCREAMING EAGLES

The 101st Airborne Division in World War II

Milton J. Shapiro

JULIAN MESSNER
NEW YORK

Published by Julian Messner,
a Division of Simon & Schuster, Inc.
1 West 39 Street, New York, N. Y. 10018. All rights reserved.

To my grandson Joshua. May all his wars be only history.

Library of Congress Cataloging in Publication Data
Shapiro, Milton J.
   The screaming eagles.
   Bibliography: p. 186
   Includes index.
   1. World War, 1939-1945—Regimental histories—United
States—101st Division. 2. United States. Army.
101st Division. I. Title.
D769.3.101st.S48   940.54′12′73   76-15568
ISBN 0-671-32808-5 lib. bdg.

Acknowledgments

The material for this book came from the Historical Records Section, Office of the Chief of Military History of the War Department. At the National Archives in Maryland and at the museum and library of the 101st at Ft. Campbell, Kentucky, the author was granted complete access to all records, combat and after-combat reports, maps, General Orders, and morning reports—anything and everything needed to compile this combat history of the Screaming Eagles Division. To the dozens of men and women, uniformed and civilian, who helped in this research, the author gives his heartfelt thanks. He is especially grateful to Lt. Col. Hugh G. Waite and Ms. Lynn Gunn-Smith, of the Office of the Chief of Information at the Pentagon, Washington, D.C.; to Mrs. Margaret Chamberlain, Public Information Officer at Ft. Campbell; and, also at Ft. Campbell, Maj. F. C. McGourty, Lt. William J. Phillips, and Master Sergeant Thomas J. Feeney.

And to my wife, Jill, who helped pen the voluminous notes needed for this research, and who drew the maps included in this book.

Other published sources were used as background information in writing this history. For a list of these sources, a selected bibliography is included.

Milton J. Shapiro

Organization of the 101st Airborne Division

The 101st Airborne Division, as with all infantry divisions of the U.S. Army at the time of World War II, was organized on the basis of the "triangle concept." That is, each unit of the division was subdivided into three smaller units, down to the smallest unit, the squad, consisting of twelve men. Thus, three squads made a platoon, three platoons a company, three companies a battalion, three battalions a regiment, and three regiments made a division.

In addition, auxiliary units went into the makeup of a division, such as artillery, engineers, military police, medics, signals, quartermaster, (supply) ordnance, graves registration, and so forth. Being an airborne division, the 101st also had its unit of glider infantry, the 327th Regiment. The parachute regiments were the 501st, the 502nd, and the 506th.

A division would be commanded by a general, either brigadier or major general. A regiment would have a Lt. Colonel or full colonel in command; a major would lead a battalion, a captain a company, a lieutenant a platoon. Of course, in combat situations, casualties might spring a junior officer into command of a larger unit temporarily, adjustment being made when the unit came out of the line for a rest.

Regiments were given numbers (501st, 327th, etc.). Battalions were simply designated 1st, 2nd, and 3rd; companies were given letters of the alphabet. In combat, to avoid confusion, especially during radio communications, the letters were given standard meanings. They were as follows: Able, Baker, and Charley Companies were in 1st Battalion; Dog, Easy, and Fox Companies were in 2nd Battalion; George, How, and Item were in 3rd Battalion.

Introduction

In late spring of 1944, the fifth year of World War II, the third year of the United States part in the conflict, the situation in the battle against Hitler's Germany stood like this:

The German forces had been driven out of North Africa. Allied forces, led by the U.S. Fifth Army, had captured Sicily, invaded Italy, and were driving toward Rome. Italy had in fact surrendered. Its dictator, Benito Mussolini, had been driven from office and arrested. Rescued from prison by a daring German paratroop raid, he'd fled to the North and was leading two Italian divisions that had remained faithful to him. Meanwhile, on the Eastern front, powerful Russian counterattacks were driving the *Wermacht*—the German Army—ever closer to the borders of its own country.

For the Allies, there remained but the raising of the final curtain of the drama—the invasion of occupied France from the springboard of England.

As early as May of 1943, a target date of May 1, 1944, had been set by the combined chiefs of Staff of the Allied Forces for the invasion across the English Channel. The operation had been code named Overlord.

When General Dwight D. Eisenhower arrived in London from Africa to take over as Supreme Commander, Allied Expeditionary Force, he and his closest aides studied the invasion plans. Eventually, Gen. Eisenhower recommended a month's delay. There were arguments against a postponement, many of them valid. But Gen. Eisenhower felt there were more good reasons for a delay than against it. The month would give the Allied air arm extra time for its attacks against such targets as bridges, railroads, and heavy gun emplacements. Furthermore, there was a shortage of landing craft; a month's delay would help fill the shortages. Finally, the Russians were waiting for a complete thaw in Poland to launch a big offensive; this would tie down German troops on that front, troops which might otherwise be diverted to defend against the invasion of France.

Operation Overlord was postponed until the first week of June. As Gen. Eisenhower knew, this was a calculated risk. Only in late spring and early summer were the Channel tides favorable for the launching of a vast invasion fleet. On only three days in each month would there be the moonlit condition necessary to the airborne invasion, which had been planned to precede the seaborne landings. Should the undependable English Channel weather act up and cause a cancellation of those early June dates, another month's delay would be flirting with disaster. Allied troops keyed up for battle would suffer a letdown. The Germans, already in preparation for the invasion, would be granted another month to prepare defenses, work on secret new weapons, and bring up new divisions.

Early in May of 1944, Gen. Eisenhower set the actual date for D-Day—the invasion day—for the fifth of June. On that day, as the official order read, Allied troops would land on the continent of Europe and, ". . . undertake operations aimed at the heart of Germany and the destruction of her armed forces."

The Germans, meanwhile, were not completely asleep. They knew the blow was coming. Exactly when, exactly where, they could not find out for sure. Spies had given them the code name of the venture: Overlord. Spies had also informed them that the British Broadcasting Corporation would tip off the French underground by code when the invasion was about to begin. But, to a large extent, neither Hitler nor his commanding generals put much stock in these intelligence reports. This was fortunate for the Allies. Fortunately, too, there was much division on the German side about the time and place of the coming invasion. Hitler himself guessed right about where the invasion would take place—the Cotentin peninsula of France. But Field Marshall Karl R. G. von Rundstedt, architect of the German sweep across France in 1940, pointed to the Pas de Calais, that part of France closest to England across the channel.

Agreeing with von Rundstedt was Field Marshall Erwin Rommel, the Desert Fox. For once Hitler's egomania gave way to advice from his army commanders—again, fortunately for the Allies. However, the two battle-hardened generals disagreed completely on the strategy for combatting the invasion. Von Rundstedt felt it would be impossible to stop the landings themselves, and insisted on a strategy of a mobile reserve, which would be rushed in where needed. On the other hand, Rommel felt that the Germans' only chance was to meet the Allied armies head on at the beaches with everything they had and drive the invaders back into the Channel. He felt that once the Allies had gained a firm foothold on the mainland, their overall superiority in the air and on the ground would crush von Rundstedt's mobile reserves.

Thus the German strategy became fragmented. Each of the two famed field marshalls managed to wring concessions from Hitler. German command and German forces were split. A portion of the German armor went to von Rundstedt, and Rommel got the rest. While von Rundstedt concerned himself with planning counterattacks after the Allied landings, Rommel began a feverish campaign of fortification and obstacle building right on the beaches and directly behind them. Shrewdly expecting an airborne attack, Rommel planted entire fields with slanting poles strung with wire as obstacles against paratroops and gliders. *Rommelsspargel*, Rommel's asparagus, his troops called the poles.

As June 5 approached, the supreme German commanders paid little heed to Hitler's warning that the invasion would hit the Cotentin peninsula. Lined up in the Pas de Calais area were nineteen divisions of the German Fifteenth Army with five divisions of the Seventh Army in reserve behind them. In Normandy, along the Cotentin peninsula, the stripped Seventh Army had but six divisions, with one division in reserve.

And then the weather intervened. On the night of June 3, with Allied convoys already beginning to rendezvous for the invasion, word came from the meteorologists that June 5 would be stormy and windy. The invasion order was cancelled; convoys were called back.

The following night, in the library of Southwick House near Portsmouth, England, as the rain fell in sheets and the wind blew in gusts off the Channel, Gen. Eisenhower faced a grim group of men. Time was running out. A decision would have to be made. A further postponement could bring on that dreaded month's delay.

Yet, the weather ruled all. The bombers flying in advance of the invasion needed reasonable weather. The paratroopers needed a moon for their night drop ahead of the seaborne troops. The Channel had to be calm enough to allow the immense fleet of ships and invasion craft to cross safely and disembark troops.

Would the capricious Channel weather behave itself on

the night of the fifth and the morning of the sixth? The grim men in the library waited expectantly now as Group Captain J. M. Stagg of the Royal Air Force began his meteorological report.

The news was encouraging. A new weather front due the next day should free the area of rain. Winds would drop, although not desist entirely. Cloud cover would rise and partly dissipate. There should be enough ceiling for the bombers to operate. And for the paratroops, there would be a moon.

A volley of eager questions from Gen. Eisenhower and his subordinates followed the briefing. But Capt. Stagg could not elaborate. He could offer no guarantees. An element of risk remained.

The decision was Gen. Eisenhower's to make, and he had very little time left in which to make it. If D-Day were to be Tuesday, the sixth of June, he would have to give the order within half an hour. Troops had to be assembled, ships refueled, a thousand and one details finalized.

He took a quick poll of the men in the room. Britain's Air Chief Marshall Sir Arthur Tedder was doubtful. Air Chief Marshall Sir Trafford Leigh-Mallory was likewise doubtful. British Field Marshall Sir Bernard L. Montgomery was eager to go. Major General Walter Bedell Smith, Gen. Eisenhower's Chief of Staff, said it was a gamble but June 6 it should be.

At 9:45 P.M. that Sunday night, June 4, Gen. Eisenhower made his decision. "I am quite positive we must give the order," he said. "I don't like it, but there it is. I don't see how we can possibly do anything else."

The invasion was on.

PART I
NORMANDY

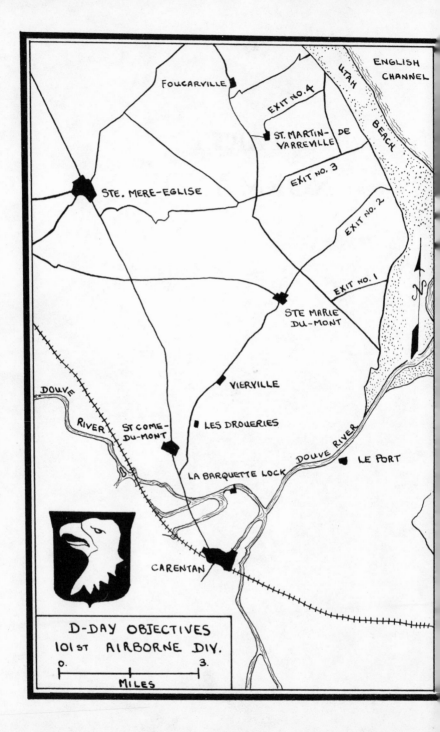

FOUCARVILLE

EXIT NO. 4

ST. MARTIN-
VARREVILLE

EXIT NO. 3

STE. MERE-EGLISE

EXIT NO. 2

EXIT NO. 1

STE MARIE
DU-MONT

ENGLISH
CHANNEL

UTAH

BEACH

N

VIERVILLE

DOUVE

RIVER

ST COME-
DU-MONT

LES DROUERIES

DOUVE RIVER

LE PORT

LA BARQUETTE LOCK

CARENTAN

D-DAY OBJECTIVES
101ST AIRBORNE DIV.
0.   3.
MILES

Chapter One

The twin engines of the C-47 transport planes sputtered into life, and, at seven different airfield staging areas in the south of England, 6,670 paratroopers of the 101st Airborne Division began to board the aircraft. The time was 2200 hours —10 P.M. The troopers' faces were blackened for camouflage, their heads shaven—some of them Mohawk Indian style—their bodies loaded with some 125 pounds of weapons, ammunition, and equipment. On their left shoulders they proudly wore the black, yellow, and white patch of their division—the Screaming Eagle.

Gen. Eisenhower, accompanied by Brigadier General Maxwell D. Taylor, Division Commander, made the rounds of the airfields in a jeep, personally saying goodbye and wishing good luck to as many men as he could. Others received his message over the loudspeakers in their aircraft.

Then the pilots of the 9th Air Force Troop Carrier Squadron revved the engines. The big planes shook and shuddered from the prop wash, then slowly began taxiing to the runways. As the last light began to fade in the western sky, the first planes in the great armada rose into the air, formed into formation, and headed for the coast of France.

By 2330 hours all 490 troop carrier planes were airborne.

They flew in V-formations of 9 planes each, 45 planes to a "serial." In each plane was a "stick" of paratroopers in varying numbers, but averaging about 14 to a "stick." Each plane had equipment bundles which would be pushed out the door before the jump. Most of the planes also carried munitions and equipment strapped to their bellies, which would be jettisoned over the drop zones.

In one of the C-47's, asleep on a mattress pad, rode Division Commander Taylor. In another rode Brig. Gen. Anthony C. McAuliffe, the division's artillery commander. In the paratroops, the generals jumped with the privates.

The mission of the 101st Airborne was to pave the way for the 4th Infantry Division, which would be landing on the morning of D-Day at the beach called Utah Beach on the invasion plans. The nature of the beach area dictated the various missions of the division's regiments. Stretching inland for about a mile was a belt of salt marsh. Dirt causeways, topped by asphalt roads, had been built across the marshes, and these provided the only convenient exits from the beach area to the solid ground west of the marsh. These four causeways were designated exits 1, 2, 3, and 4. Near Exit 4, just west of the village of St.-Martin-de-Varreville, stood a four-gun German coastal battery that posed an ominous threat to the landings on Utah Beach.

To the men of the 502nd Regiment went the job of destroying the coastal battery and the artillery garrison nearby, setting up roadblocks northward, at Foucarville, to prevent enemy reinforcements from reaching the beach area, and finally capturing causeways 3 and 4 and securing them for the infantry.

Causeways 1 and 2 were to be captured by the 506th Regiment. These troopers were also ordered to set up roadblocks at Vierville and Ste. Marie-du-Mont and to capture or destroy two wooden bridges over the Douve River, two miles northeast of the town of Carentan. The 506th, being on the extreme left of the division, was to secure that flank against enemy attack, and provide a link between its parent unit, the VIIth Corps, and the neighboring Vth Corps coming up off Omaha Beach.

The remaining parachute regiment, the 501st, was given the job of capturing the locks at La Barquette and destroying the railroad bridge and four highway bridges northwest of Carentan. Destruction of the bridges was vital in stopping German reinforcements from entering the Utah Beach area. As for the locks, these were being used by the Germans to flood the area inland from the beach, except for the causeways. Once the Germans realized the invasion was on, they could flood the causeways, too, effectively sealing the 4th Division into its beachhead. The 501st had to seize and hold these locks against counterattacks until the men of the 4th came through.

That night of June 5, 1944, enemy ground forces were not on full alert. They, too, had seen the weather reports, and had discounted the possibility of an invasion until later in the month. Field Marshall Rommel, in fact, had gone home on leave the day before. Several other high ranking German commanders had left their posts and departed for Rennes, for a war game exercise. In St. Lô, a midnight birthday party for Gen. Erich Marcks was just getting under way.

The Allied commanders could not know this, of course. In any case, they had formulated their own plans to confuse the enemy, keep him off balance, keep him guessing. Instead of flying the 101st Airborne directly to its drop zones in Normandy, a circular route was worked out. The skytrain of C-47's was to fly out of England in a wide arc, head for the Channel Islands of Guernsey and Jersey, then make an almost 90-degree left turn, come in over the French coast on the west side of the Cherbourg Peninsula, drop the troopers, and then continue to complete the circle over the Channel and back to England. To avoid enemy radar, they were ordered to fly over the water "on the deck," at only 500 feet.

And so the great air armada flew into the darkness, skimming the white caps. Meanwhile, on the ground of occupied France, only minutes ahead of the troopers, things were already happening.

The Pathfinders had dropped into action. Just after midnight a gallant band of some 120 paratroop volunteers, under the command of Capt. Frank L. Lillyman, had begun dropping on the Cotentin area. All had not gone well. The Dakota transports had encountered fog, then German antiaircraft fire. Some of the planes broke formation, lost their bearings, and dropped their men miles from the intended drop zones. One plane was forced to ditch in the Channel.

But at 0015 hours—12:15 A.M., Jumpmaster Lillyman tumbled into space to become the first American soldier to land on occupied French soil. Lillyman and his 18-man stick were dropped on a field near St. Germain-de-Varreville, about a mile and half from their target zone. Landing in the pitch blackness, an unlighted cigar between his teeth, Lillyman scurried around trying to find the rest of his men. For identification purposes in the darkness, the troopers were equipped with metal toy "crickets." A click-clack signalled a fellow trooper. The troopers also could challenge in the darkness with the password, "Flash!" The reply had to be, "Thunder."

So Lillyman hit the ground, cut away his parachute harness, and began moving about in the blackness, quietly searching, listening. A dark shape loomed ahead of him, moving slowly. He click-clacked. No reply. Another click-clack. The shape moved, but still no reply. Lillyman reached for a grenade. The Pathfinders had been warned to avoid firing their weapons, to avoid encounters with the enemy.

They had more important things to do. But now Lillyman felt he had no choice. He began to pull the pin from his grenade when the shape uttered a low, friendly, "Moo." Lillyman had landed in a cow pasture.

He had to move quickly now. Time was of the essence. He could find only about 40 men from the Pathfinder group. The rest were either lost, killed, or captured. The 40 would have to do the work of a 120. From the outset they had been divided into three sections, one for each of the three 101st drop zones. Carrying lights, luminous panels, flares, and radios, the mission of the Pathfinders was to light and call the way in for the main body of the Screaming Eagles. The lights and panels were so designed that they could be seen easily from the air, but not by men on the ground.

The lead pilots of the transports were instructed to home-in on these lights, which were colored amber, red, and green for the various elements of the division. The lights were to be laid out in the shape of a T, the crossbar indicating the "Go" point.

As Lillyman and his brave small group swung into action, gingerly stepping around enemy patrols, the Screaming Eagles began to cross the coast of France. And suddenly the night sky exploded around them.

The C-47's were flying at 1500 feet now, to avoid small arms fire from the ground. But it was not small arms fire they met, or had to fear. The German antiaircraft guns along the coast opened up with everything they had. Huge searchlight beams probed the sky, picked out the transports, and pinned them like helpless moths. Flares and rockets exploded in and around the formations, lighting up the night in a terrible and deadly Fourth of July display.

The big guns opened up. The flak bursts sent killing shards of steel through the fragile skins of the transports. Thousands of machine gun tracers stitched red and orange patterns in the blackness, tore holes in the wings and the bodies of the planes, and too often in the bodies of the helpless troopers. The C-47's rocked and shuddered under the tremendous impact of the explosions. They bucked and swerved like frightened, stricken birds. Gaunt-faced troopers stood up and hooked up their parachute lines.

This was for real. This was it. The months and months of training and waiting were over. Outside, below, there was an enemy trying to kill them. The troopers wanted out, wanted their feet on the ground and weapons in hand to defend themselves.

With just minutes to go to the target zones, many of the C-47 pilots began to panic. Never before had they experienced anything so terrifying. Though under orders to take no evasive action, lest they drop the troopers off target, the pilots began violent maneuvers to avoid the deadly ack-ack fire. Some turned away, some climbed higher, others dropped to almost treetop level. The maneuvering planes forced others out of formation. The smooth V's broke up; soon C-47's were scattered helter-skelter all over the Peninsula.

The troopers jammed in the planes had no way of knowing this was going on. Some of them, standing up in aircraft that had their doors removed, could see the awful pyrotechnics in the sky around them. They could even sense a strange, eerie, frightening beauty in the display of deadly fireworks. But the beauty was soon lost when a trooper was hit and cried out in pain, or slumped, silent and lifeless, to the floor.

Now the red light winked on in the transports; the two-minute warning light. "Check your equipment!" came the cry from the jumpmaster. Each man in the stick checked out the man directly in front of him. The last man in the stick turned around and let the man in front of him make the check. Then each man doublechecked his own hookup from the static line on his chute to the cable running overhead on the aircraft's ceiling. When he jumped, this 15-foot long static line would pull the chute from its pack automatically; they would be coming in too low—at 700 feet—to risk a free fall jump.

As each man checked the equipment, he called out, depending on his place in the stick, "Fourteen OK . . . Thirteen OK . . . Twelve OK . . ." and so on down the line.

Then came the order, "Stand in the door!" The jump-master went to the open doorway. Behind him the other troopers shuffled closer together, straining to keep their balance in the bucking, rocking transports. The flak intensified. A C-47 got a direct hit, staggered, fell off on one wing, caught fire, and plunged to earth like a dying meteor. Another C-47 was blown to bits as a flak burst caught the supply of demolition equipment strapped to its belly.

The green light came on. "Let's go!" screamed the jump-master, pushing an equipment bundle through the door and following it out. Behind him the rest of the men took their turns in the doorway. Then it was step out the door, a quick turn to the left; step out the door, a quick turn to the right —all the way down the line.

Two seconds . . . perhaps three . . . the static line caught, tore the chute from its pack. The canopy hissed and crackled as it opened, and jerked the trooper's body as it unfurled and caught the air.

Every man had his orders to jump unless he had broken limbs or severe body wounds. No man wanted to remain behind. Wounded men jumped. Some men who shouldn't have, jumped. In one plane the jumpmaster was hit. His body blocked the doorway. He was pushed out of the plane.

The drop was chaotic. By now the planes were so widely dispersed that a coherent drop was impossible. Some pilots, hopelessly lost, accidently dropped their men in the Channel. Weighed down by equipment, the men drowned. Other pilots, "hedgehopping" to avoid the antiaircraft fire, dropped their men from only 200 or 300 feet. The troopers from these planes hit the ground and died before their chutes had a chance to open.

The men were dropped haphazardly into streams, into swamps, onto fields and gardens, and into the midst of towns. They dropped into trees and onto rooftops. Some were dropped smack in the middle of enemy troop formations. Some 1,500 men of the 101st were dropped completely out of the eight-square-mile zone designated for the jump. Most of these men were killed or captured soon after hitting the ground.

The units lost all semblance of cohesion. Even the two airborne divisions were mixed. Some paratroops of the 82nd Airborne, targeted to the north and west around the key town of Ste. Mère-Église, landed in 101st territory, and some of the Screaming Eagles landed in the 82nd drop zone. In the darkness, in the confusion, it quickly seemed as though Normandy had been invaded by a plague of crickets. Troopers signalled to each other frantically with their metal toys, searching for buddies, and for their officers. Men began to gather in small groups among the thick hedgerows, in the deep ditches. In two's and three's, sometimes in groups of ten or fifteen, these determined bands of troopers, well briefed on their missions, formed themselves into independent combat teams.

Small private wars began to erupt as the troopers ran into German patrols. By now the *Wermacht* had been alerted to the drop. The German field commanders were still unsure of the paratroopers' purpose. They couldn't know whether the air drop was meant as a feint, a diversion, or a commando attack, or whether it was indeed the prelude to a full scale invasion by sea.

Nevertheless the cries of alarm were now being heard on field telephones all over Normandy.

"Fallschirmjager! Fallschirmjager! Paratroops!"

Chapter Two

The American paratroopers were not alone in their confusion. The scattering of the 101st and 82nd Airborne Divisions all over the landscape caused sheer pandemonium in the ranks of the Germans. While frantic messages went out to Rommel in Germany, to the war games meeting in Rennes, and to St. Lô, where the wine was flowing freely, the *Wermacht* officers on the scene desperately tried to make some sense out of the situation. Their maps were littered with the markings of reported parachute drops. The Americans seemed to be everywhere—as indeed they were. The attacks were coming from all directions at once, but to the German commanders, no plan appeared to be developing. What was the mission of these paratroopers? How many were there? The Germans hadn't a clue.

The troopers, for their part, recovered quickly. In spite of their dispersion, despite the lack of control, the Screaming Eagles picked themselves up and got moving. The unique individuality of the American soldier soon asserted itself in aggressive action. The troopers knew what they were there for and what they had to do. They set about doing it.

At about 2 A.M., Capt. Cleveland Fitzgerald, commanding officer, B Company, 1st Battalion of the 502nd, found himself with one of his platoon leaders, Lt. Harold Hoggard, and nine enlisted men. The mission of the 1st Battalion was to take the town of Foucarville and secure the right flank of the 101st by setting up roadblocks north of the town. The battalion was scattered to the winds. Some of the men had landed too far north of the town, right in the middle of an enemy strongpoint, and had been taken prisoner.

Capt. Fitzgerald couldn't wait for the battalion to form. He took his ten men and advanced into Foucarville. The captain led the way. In the darkness, they blundered into the German command post. Fitzgerald turned into a courtyard. A German sentry spotted him and fired. The captain went down, badly wounded—but even in falling, he triggered his submachine gun, killing the sentry. Then he yelled to the other men, "Don't come up!"

Lt. Hoggard sent a man forward to look Fitzgerald over. Ducking bullets, hugging a stone wall, the man made it to the captain's side. Fitzgerald said to him, "Tell Hoggard not to bother with me. I'm dying."

There was little Hoggard could do. He had no medics in his little band and the small arms fire was too heavy to risk sending men in to carry the captain out. He decided to let Capt. Fitzgerald lie there. He withdrew his squad of men about 700 yards and waited for daylight.

Other troopers filtered through the fields and joined Hoggard. At first light he had twenty-five men with him. He now felt strong enough to attack the village once more. He sent out two scouts, PFC. William Emerson and Pvt. Orville J. Hamilton. They reached Fitzgerald without drawing enemy fire. "Leave me alone, keep going!" Fitzgerald ordered them. The scouts advanced through the buildings and ran into two other troopers. One was a sergeant, who had entered the village from the other end.

Suddenly a shower of grenades fell around the four men and machine gun fire raked the square. Hamilton was hit in the back. Sgt. Olin L. Howard was hit in the wrist. Working under fire, the other two men gave them first aid, then helped them back to where Capt. Fitzgerald was lying.

Hoggard and his group, moving in behind the scouts, had also taken heavy machine gun fire. But they captured two prisoners who told them the fire was coming from the hill just outside of town. There were some 150 enemy dug in on the hill. Hoggard then withdrew his small force, taking the wounded along. Except for Capt. Fitzgerald, who was too badly wounded to be moved.

At about 6 A.M. Hoggard and his group made it back to the Battalion forward Command Post, which Maj. Thomas A. Sutliffe had set up just to the west of Foucarville. There was a medic at the CP, so Hoggard took four men and went back to rescue Fitzgerald. Blood plasma was given to the captain on the spot. Then, with the aid of a meat cart, Hoggard got him back to the command post. (Capt. Fitzgerald survived, only to lose his life in a car accident in Germany after the war.)

While the action around Foucarville was for the moment stalemated, Lt. Col. Pat J. Cassidy, 1st Battalion's commanding officer, was setting up his command post about half a mile south of Foucarville, with a mixed group of men. Shortly after hitting the ground, Cassidy had run into Pathfinder commander Frank Lillyman, who had given him the good news that the coastal battery had been completely bombed out. Cassidy sent Lillyman out to establish a roadblock south of Foucarville, still unaware of Fitzgerald's attack there. Then, just as dawn was breaking, he led his group on an attack against the objective known as W-X-Y-Z—the artillery barracks near the gun position. The guns might have been bombed out, but the barracks area was still thick with Germans.

A squad of troopers charged at the first building. They

found no enemy, and Col. Cassidy took it over as his command post. Later, it was learned that two Germans had been concealed in the building all day. The landlady told Cassidy that the Germans had been kind to her, and she had helped them hide.

At the gun position itself, Cassidy found Lt. Col. Steve A. Chappuis, CO of the 2nd Battalion. Destruction of the gun had been part of the 2nd's job. The Air Force had done the job for them, but for the moment Chappuis decided to wait at the position for more of his men to turn up. Cassidy went back to his CP. There he was told that the men attacking the barracks complex had run into a stiff fight. There wasn't too much Cassidy could do about that. He needed what few men he had to protect his base and to man the roadblocks he'd been setting up. He had no way of knowing who or what was around him—friends or enemy. But he finally dispatched fifteen men under Staff Sgt. Harrison Summers to help the attack at the barracks.

Summers did not get an easy job. He was leading a mixed group of men who had never worked together before. He didn't know even one man from his detail. The buildings he was ordered to attack were of thick stone, with firing slits hacked out by the enemy like the forts of American frontier days.

Sgt. Summers figured the only way to attack was go in himself and hope the others would follow his example. He simply walked up to the first house and kicked the door in. The Germans inside were busily firing through the slits at the men outside. They didn't see Summers until he was already inside, blasting away with his Tommy gun. Four Germans dropped. The rest fled.

Summers emerged from the building, looking for his other men. They were under cover in a ditch alongside the road near the houses. Saying nothing to them, Summers crawled through a hedge and dashed into a second house. This was empty. Now, as Summers headed for the third house, Pvt. William A. Burt rose from the ditch and set up his light machine gun to cover him. Burt fired at the house. The Germans replied with rifles and machine pistols, but, firing at the ports, Burt made the Germans keep their heads down. Their return fire was wild.

Summers headed for the door. Suddenly, he was joined by Lt. Elmer F. Brandenberger, from Summers' own B Company. As they sprinted for the door, a machine gun burst almost ripped off Brandenberger's arm, knocking him down. Summers charged in alone, firing as he came through the door. There were six Germans inside. Summers shot them all down with one sweep of his Tommy gun.

As Summers moved to the next house, a captain from the 82nd Airborne joined him. Before they had advanced twenty yards, a sniper cut down the captain. Summers never even had a chance to learn the man's name. Shot through the heart, the captain died instantly. Again Summers went in alone. Six more Germans fell before his Tommy gun.

Summers got a little help now. Aside from Pvt. Burt, who continued to keep the Germans busy with his light machine gun, there was Pvt. John Camien. As the 82nd Airborne captain fell, Camien rose from the ditch, armed with an M1 carbine, and joined Summers in the clean-out. The two men worked over five stone houses, killing thirty Germans. They took turns, switching weapons back and forth. One man went in with the Tommy gun, while the other covered him with the carbine.

Then, beyond the last house, the two men rushed a long low building. Summers kicked the door open and rushed in. It proved to be the Germans' mess hall. Incredibly, fifteen men were sitting at the tables, eating, paying no attention to the fighting going on around them. As the Germans started to rise, Summers swept the table with his submachine gun and killed all of them.

For his gallant action at the barracks area, Summers won a field commission and was awarded the Distinguished Service Cross.

But the fight at W-X-Y-Z was not quite finished. Not yet. There was still one large double-storied house to clean out. Summers and Camien led the rest of the group against this building, with Burt moving up along the road with his machine gun. The men worked their way up to a thick hedgerow. At this point a flat open field lay between them and that last house. As the group began to deploy along the hedgerow, a German sniper began to pick them off, one by one.

The men got up and charged across the field. The Germans fired from the ports, while from the right flank more sniper fire raked the open field. Four men fell dead. Four others were wounded. Dragging the wounded back, the men retreated to the hedgerow. They'd have to try something else.

Next to the big stone building was a wooden shed and a haystack. Burt fired tracer bullets at the haystack. It went up in flames, the fire spreading to the shed. Then the shed, which had been used for storing ammunition, began to explode like a volcano. Some Germans ran out. The troopers cut them down. At that point Staff Sergeant Roy Nickrent got into the action. Col. Cassidy had sent him forward with a bazooka to see what he could do. Nickrent, figuring the stone walls of the building were too much for his weapon, aimed for the roof. He fired off a couple of rounds for range, then began hitting his target. Smoke curled from the building. The Germans inside ran from it—and were caught in a murderous crossfire.

On one side were Summers and his group. At the same time, crossing through an orchard north of Summers, came leading elements of the 4th Division. These men had landed at Utah Beach earlier and had moved safely across the causeways secured by the 101st. And, from the west, moving down the road, was a team from the 502nd Regimental Headquarters Company, led by Lt. Col. John Michaelis.

All three groups zeroed in on the fleeing Germans. About fifty of the enemy were killed; the remainder, about thirty, raised their hands and yelled, *"Kamerad!"* Summers and his men took over the last house, sat down, and took five minutes off for a smoke.

While Cassidy's 1st Battalion was fighting around the artillery barracks, the 3rd Battalion, under Lt. Col. Robert G. Cole, was launching its attack on Causeways 3 and 4, preparatory to the 4th Division landings. Soon after dropping, Col. Cole picked up Maj. J.W. Vaughn, Capt. George A. Buker, and two enlisted men. As they moved out, stragglers attached themselves to the party. Few of these new men were from Col. Cole's regiment. They came from the 506th and from the 82nd Airborne, which wasn't too surprising, considering that the colonel had been wrongly dropped near Ste. Mère-Eglise, an 82nd target.

Getting his bearings, Col. Cole moved out, picked up some more men, and headed for St. Martin-de-Varreville, near the German coastal battery and Causeway No. 4. At a crossroads the group ran into an enemy convoy of five carts hauling mines and equipment. There was a short, furious engagement. Several Germans were killed, and ten were captured, along with the equipment. But Maj. Vaughn, who was the regimental supply officer, was killed by a machine gun burst, and Lt. Leroy Bone, the demolitions officer, was also killed.

With about 80 men now in his group, Col. Cole went on. He sent Lt. Robert G. Burns of Company I southward, to make contact with the 506th; Capt. Robert L. Clements of

Company G to Causeway 4; and he himself led a group to clear out Causeway 3. Fighting was already going on around these upper two causeways. Scattered groups of troopers had been dropped in the vicinity and had been engaging the enemy during the early hours of the morning. By 7:30 on D-Day morning, 4th Division troops began pushing German units off the beach areas and onto the causeways. At No. 3, Cole and men dug in, and calmly picked off the retreating Germans as they came through. They killed 75 this way, without losing a man. At 1300 hours (1 P.M.) they made contact with the 8th Regiment of the 4th Division. Causeways 3 and 4 were secured.

Gen. Taylor, commanding general of the 101st, landed in a field of cows on his drop. His plan had been to form a division headquarters in the vicinity of the town of Hiesville, and from there to direct the battle. But of immediate concern to Gen. Taylor was the securing of the four causeways —the four exits from the beaches needed by the 4th Division. In the first hour or so after his drop, the general had collected a group of key officers and some troopers. But he hadn't any news at all of the 506th, the regiment which should have landed near him, and whose mission was the securing of Causeways 1 and 2.

It was apparent to Gen. Taylor that the 506th had been dropped far out of position. Equally obvious to him was the fact that with H-Hour of D-Day approaching, he'd better see to clearing those causeways himself. He had collected some troopers of the 501st, his artillery commander, Brig. Gen. Anthony C. McAuliffe, with some artillerymen, Lt. Col. Julian J. Ewell, CO of the 3rd Battalion, 501st, Col. Higgins, division Chief of Staff, and several other senior officers.

The time was just before first light. At that moment, and in that vicinity, 52 gliders of the 101st Airborne began their descent. The gliders carried 16 antitank guns (57mm), engineers, a bulldozer, signal equipment, a medical company with portable field hospital, a radio-equipped jeep for Gen. Taylor, and an assortment of 148 men. In the lead glider was Brig. Gen. Donald F. Pratt, the assistant division commander.

The gliders, towed by C-47's, ran into troubles similar to those experienced by the troopers. Flak scattered some of the planes. Some of the pilots missed their zones and cut the tow-ropes either too early or too late. Many of the gliders crash landed, to be torn apart in the hedgerows or by Rommel's Asparagus—the field obstacles. Gen. Pratt was killed when his glider skidded across a field slippery with dew and crashed into the trees.

Nevertheless, most of the men got out safely, and much of the equipment was saved. Gen. Taylor sent Col. Thomas L. Sherburne with Capt. Cecil Wilson and ten men to collect the men from the gliders and move them on to Hiesville. He would join them later, after seeing to the causeways.

With so few men, Gen. Taylor realized he could not take and hold more than one of the exits. He chose No. 1, and gave Col. Ewell command of the attack force. The colonel's own 3rd Battalion had been badly scattered during the jump. Three of its planes had been shot down. Just after dawn, some eighty-five men began to move down the road. There were sixty men from Ewell's unit, plus about twenty-five men from Division Headquarters, including the two generals, MP's, clerks, staff officers, even Robert Reuben, the war correspondent from Reuters, the British news agency. Reuben was the only newsman to jump with the paratroopers.

It was a strange group indeed. Major Larry Legere led a squad. Lieutenants were acting as scouts. There were so many senior officers about that Gen. Taylor said, paraphrasing a famous Winston Churchill remark, "Never were so few led by so many."

Moving along in columns on either side of the road, with scouts and flankers out, the force encountered harassing fire from ditches and hedgerows along the road. The scouts and troopers routed out the Germans without loss. One of the scouts, Corp. Vergil Danforth, shot dead four of the Germans. Another scout got two more, and the rest ran.

Near Ste. Marie-du-Mont more troopers drifted in and joined the group. Unsure of his exact position, Gen. Taylor, who spoke excellent French, stopped at a farmhouse and asked directions. He was told that the nearest town was Pouppeville. Gen. Taylor told Col. Ewell to take the town, which lay astride Causeway No. 1.

As the force approached the town, it was fired upon from some outlying buildings. Major Legere took his squad up to flush out the Germans. A sniper's bullet caught him in the leg and he went down. Bullets kicked up around him. A cry went up: "Medic!" Ignoring the danger, T/5 Edwin Hohl rose from a ditch and raced to the major's side. Despite the Red Cross armbands on Hohl's uniform, the sniper shot him dead. The scouts discovered where the firing was coming from, returned the fire, and silenced the sniper. The column got moving again. Major Legere was moved to the safety of a roadside ditch and another medic attended to his leg wound.

The troopers moved into the town, the Germans retreating before them, finally gathering in a schoolhouse for a last-ditch defense. Col. Ewell, firing his .45 pistol, stuck his head around the corner of a building. A sniper bounded a bullet off his helmet, denting it, but not penetrating. Another sniper in a tree near the school killed Lt. Nathan Marks and two more men before the troopers got him.

Finally, a German officer came running out of the school-house and surrendered his men inside. A few other Germans began to run toward the beach area. Suddenly they saw the infantrymen of the 4th Division moving in, led by a tank. The remaining Germans threw up their arms and surrendered also.

But where, Gen. Taylor wondered, were the men of the 506th? Badly scattered. Only ten of the 81 planes carrying this regiment dropped their sticks in the correct zone. And those ten planes were filled for the most part with regimental headquarters men, whereas the capture of Causeways 1 and 2 had been assigned to the 1st and 2nd Battalions.

Col. Robert F. Sink, the regimental commander, landed near his target, but found himself entirely without his communications section. Later it was learned that all of them had dropped far outside their zones, some as far as twenty miles away. Every man had been either killed or captured.

By two in the morning, Col. Sink had gathered round him 40 men of regimental headquarters. He had also made contact with Lt. Col. William L. Turner, who was busy trying to collect his 1st Battalion in the darkness. But of the 2nd and 3rd Battalions, Col. Sink knew nothing. He moved his little group into Culoville and set up his command post. Then, with no other option left him, he sent Lt. Col. Turner and the 50 men he'd collected to Causeway 1. This was originally the job of Lt. Col. Robert L. Strayer's 2nd Battalion. Unknown to everybody, Strayer was stuck farther north, near Foucarville and Causeway No. 4, battling German infantry and artillery.

By the time Turner and his men got to Causeway 1, they found that Col. Ewell's men had already secured this exit. They returned to Culoville and reported to Col. Sink.

Col. Strayer had been dropped near St. Germain-de-Varreville, in the 502nd zone. He spent the first hour or so trying to round up his men. In a field he ran into Lt. Col. Cassidy. For the moment the two battalion commanders decided to join forces. But when they had collected about 200 men, most of them from the 506th, Strayer wanted to split and get his men moving south toward their own objective.

"Okay then," Cassidy agreed. "Clear your men out and I'll get going." Cassidy headed for the gun battery and the artillery barracks at that point, and Strayer took off. In a few minutes he ran into a large force of his own troopers, led by Capt. Clarence Hester and Lt. Lewis Nixon. By dawn Strayer had 200 men with him, and he set out for Causeways 1 and 2.

They got as far as a small town called Le Grand-Chemin when they were stopped by machine gun and heavy artillery fire. A battery of the dreaded German 88's had spotted them. Lt. Richard Winters of E Company was sent in to knock out the enemy gun positions. A task much easier said than done. Winters went in with thirteen men equipped with two machine guns, rifles, and grenades. Placing one of his machine guns to give him covering fire, he moved the other into a hedgerow facing one of the 88's. Then, splitting his little force into two groups, Winters attacked.

He charged the enemy positions, several men at his side, their weapons firing. Then they threw grenades into the trenches. The Germans fired back. One man dropped. Then another. Winters spotted two Germans setting up a machine gun. Winters squeezed off two shots from his M1. Both German gunners went down. Three more Germans began to run away from the 88. Pvt. Gerald Loraine got one, Winters the other two.

One 88 position cleaned out. Three to go. Running low on ammunition, Winters went back and got some. He also picked up two more men, and ordered his two machine guns to move in closer. Then he attacked the remaining three gun positions, killing altogether fifteen of the enemy and capturing twelve. Of his own men, four were dead and six wounded. While he had cleaned out the gun positions, he now began receiving heavy machine gun fire from some stone buildings nearby. This was too much for his small group. He pulled the men back. Then he slipped down to the beach area, where the 4th Division was landing, brought back two tanks from the 70th Tank Battalion, and completed his job of destroying the 88 positions.

Lt. Winters was awarded the DSC for that morning's work.

While the German 88 battery was being attacked, Col. Strayer pulled out the men from D Company and sent them down to Causeway No. 2. Fighting small skirmishes with German patrols all the way, D Company reached the causeway about 1:30 A.M. and brought it under control.

A substantial portion of the 101st's D-Day mission was thus far accomplished. The four causeways leading off Utah Beach were secured. Men, tanks, and equipment were moving over these causeways inland. The coastal battery and the artillery barracks had been destroyed. Roadblocks had been set up outside Fourcarville to secure the right flank of the division and prevent enemy reinforcements from moving south toward the invasion beaches.

But the division was still badly scattered. There still remained the mission of capturing the locks at La Barquette, the destruction of railroad and highway bridges northwest of Carentan, and the destruction or capture of the two wooden bridges over the Douve.

There was much hard fighting yet to be done.

Chapter Three

The 3rd Battalion of the 506th, whose job it was to take the two wooden bridges over the Douve, dropped into a hornets' nest. Their zone was one of the very few spots in Normandy where the Germans had anticipated a parachute attack. The fields were ringed with mortars and machine guns. As the first troopers began to drop, the Germans set aflame an oil-soaked house, lighting up the entire area. Twenty troopers were killed before they hit the ground. The Battalion commander, Lt. Col. Robert L. Wolverton, his executive officer, and one of the company commanders were all killed in the ambush. The other company commanders were immediately captured. One of them, Capt. Robert Harwick, escaped two days later and eventually was given command of the battalion.

One officer who survived the jump was Capt. Charles G. Shettle, a battalion staff officer. He was fortunate enough to have been dropped outside the target zone, and so escaped the ambush. He headed for the rendezvous. When he found nobody there, he continued on to Angoville-au-Plain. On the way, two more officers and thirteen enlisted men joined him, then another group of two officers and sixteen enlisted men.

This "battalion" of five officers and twenty-nine enlisted men moved out toward the bridges, fighting a series of small skirmishes on the way. About 4:30 that morning they reached the river. Another twenty men joined them. The troopers dug in and began to put fire on the Germans across the river. The Germans answered with machine guns, mortars, and artillery. The Germans had the advantage of higher ground. They put snipers into the trees and began to pick off the troopers. Lt. T.M. Chambliss of Company H stood up to rally his men. A sniper killed him with two shots in the head.

Capt. Shettle reasoned that a bridgehead on the other side of the river would effectively counter some of the German fire. He asked for volunteers. PFC. Donald Zahn and PFC. George Montilio stepped forward. Shettle sent Zahn over first. Ducking and dodging machine gun and rifle fire, Zahn dashed across the bridge, carrying a light machine gun. On the other side of the river he dived into a ditch and waved Montilio forward. Montilio ran across with the ammunition. Quickly the two men set up the machine gun and began pouring fire into the German positions.

Then Lt. Ken Christianson and Lt. Rudolph E. Bolte each led five-man patrols to the other side. Since it was now almost daylight, the men crossed on the underside of the bridge, climbing hand over hand along the girders. Finally, Lt. Richard Meason led another group across in this same fashion, Zahn and Montilio firing short bursts to keep the Germans' heads down.

On the far bank, the men deployed for an attack. Zahn and Montilio were running a bit low on ammunition, but the Germans didn't know that. The two men continued to pepper the enemy positions with short bursts as their buddies snaked forward over the ground. When they got to grenade throwing distance the Eagles attacked, knocking out three machine gun nests and killing thirteen Germans.

The bridgehead proved impossible to hold, however. The

Germans were able to bring up reinforcements, and began to zero in on the troopers with mortar and artillery fire. Zahn's machine gun was just about out of ammunition. The men were eventually forced to pull back across the bridge, covered by fire from Capt. Shettle and his men. There they redeployed, ready to repel any German counterattack.

As the morning wore on, Shettle's situation looked bleak. He sent a few two-man patrols out to look for equipment bundles. His men needed food, ammunition, and medical supplies. Some of these patrols did get back with supplies. Others were picked off by German snipers. Then a small patrol reached him from La Barquette and told him that Col. Howard "Skeets" Johnson was about a mile and a half west, holding the locks. Shettle went back with the patrol and asked Johnson for help. Johnson had to turn him down. His own forces were too meager, and he was locked in a tough battle with the Germans over control of the vital locks.

With Col. Johnson was a Lt. Farrell of First Army, who had taken special training with the Navy in directing supporting gunfire from warships. Through Farrell's radio, Shettle was able to send a message to Gen. Taylor, asking for reinforcements and equipment. The message never reached division headquarters, but, returning to his men at the wooden bridges, Shettle didn't know that yet. He was encouraged by the fact that he'd been able to get through to the Navy via radio. Later that day, forty more stragglers arrived at his position, carrying supply bundles with ammunition and rations.

Shettle was now prepared to fight it out and hold his positions. As a safeguard, he sent a demolition team in to wire the bridges. Working under the cover of darkness, the engineers set up their charges. If the Germans counterattacked and threatened to dislodge Shettle's group, the bridges would be blown up to prevent reinforcements from pouring over in any great strength.

At the time Capt. Shettle went to the locks at La Barquette to seek help, he was surprised to find Col. Johnson there, leading the 1st Battalion of the 501st into action. He was soon apprised of the reason. Though he was in fact the regimental commander, Col. Johnson took over the 1st Battalion because there was nobody else there to lead. Lt. Col. Robert C. Carroll and two of his staff officers of the 1st Battalion were killed in a German ambush shortly after landing. Maj. Philip S. Gage, Jr., the battalion exec, was wounded by machine gun fire and captured, and all the battalion's company commanders were missing. In fact, only eighteen of the forty-five planes carrying Johnson's 1st Battalion dropped their men on target.

Thus the colonel put himself in charge of this battalion, gathered together such men as he could find, and headed for the battalion's objective, the vital locks at La Barquette. Picking his way through the marshland, fighting off small enemy forces that pricked at his group like swarms of deadly mosquitoes, Johnson approached within attacking range with a force of about 150 men.

Johnson sent fifty men forward in a rush. The men had to cross open ground about the size of a football field. Much to their surprise, only a few scattered shots were fired at them. They reached the locks and captured them with no casualties. The men dug in and were well emplaced by the time the Germans began to blast them with mortar and 88 fire.

Encouraged by the ease with which he had taken the locks, Col. Johnson felt he could advance up river and complete the regiment's other mission, the destruction of the highway and railroad bridges near Carentan. These were just about a mile from his position at the locks. He sent several small patrols out to test the enemy's strength.

No sooner had these patrols left the safety of their positions then the Germans opened up. Machine gun fire swept the roads, which were built atop of dikes around the locks. Mortars and artillery shells exploded around the men. One group, led by Lt. James H. Petersen, waded neck deep through a swamp to avoid the fire-swept roads. But the patrol was caught by an 88 barrage. Peterson and many of his men were killed.

It soon became apparent to Col. Johnson that the bridges were well defended. He would need a stronger force than he then commanded. Of the whereabouts of his 2nd Battalion he knew nothing. His 3rd Battalion had been dropped along with Gen. Taylor, as regimental reserve. He didn't know where they were either. The fact was that all the morning of D-Day the colonel had no radio contact with anybody. He had no idea where anybody else was, what they were doing, or even if the D-Day landings had been successful. Like most of the Screaming Eagle units during the first hours of fighting, Col. Johnson fought his own independent war.

While he was mulling over his situation at the locks, Col. Johnson was informed that Maj. R. J. Allen, one of his staff officers, had collected a group of men from various outfits and was fighting in the town of Addeville, about three-quarters of a mile away. Leaving most of his men at the locks, he took fifty troopers and set out for Addeville, reaching the town about nine o'clock in the morning. He found Maj. Allen there with some 100 men, and Lt. Farrell, the forward observer for the Navy. Maj. Allen had his men well organized, though they were pick-ups from virtually every battalion in the division. He even had an aid station set up in a farm building, under the command of regimental surgeon Maj. Francis E. Carrel.

Col. Johnson needed more men at the locks. He told Allen to remain in Addeville, leaving him 30 men. The rest, including a team of demolition experts, he organized for a move back to La Barquette. Just then a radioman reported that Lt. Col. Robert Ballard, CO of the 2nd Battalion, was about a half mile away, at Les Droueries, fighting a pitched battle with about 250 men under his command. Col. Johnson immediately made contact with Ballard and ordered him to disengage and join him in an attack on the bridges.

But Col. Ballard was pinned down. He was heavily engaged, and enemy troops in large numbers were between him and Addeville. To try to break out would have been suicide. Johnson told him to break out as soon as he could and join with the 1st Battalion at La Barquette. Then Col. Johnson moved out with his men, on the road back to the locks.

Except for some sniping, the march back was quiet. Unknown to Col. Johnson, however, the Germans had been observing his every movement. At an intersection near the locks, soon to be called "Hell's Corners," the Germans let go a terrifying barrage. Mortars, 88's, and machine guns ranged in on the intersection. Men were cut down like wheat before a scythe. They scrambled into ditches, trying to escape the deadly rain of lead and steel.

Col. Johnson was in a quandary. If he stayed, he and his men would be wiped out; he had nothing with which to combat mortars and artillery. On the other hand, the position around the intersection was so exposed that if he tried to get his men up and out, he faced annihilation just the same.

Then he remembered the lieutenant and the Navy. Crawling on his belly as bullets and shrapnel tore the air and earth around him, Col. Johnson found Lt. Farrell. In a few minutes the lieutenant had raised the U.S.S. *Quincy* on the radio. The cruiser was just off the coast. Soon huge eight-inch shells were screaming overhead, blasting the German positions. Operating under incredibly difficult circumstances, for he had to keep ducking enemy fire, Lt. Farrell nonetheless was able to direct the naval gunfire, adjust it via his radio, and get the salvos right on target.

The German fire faded away. Col. Johnson was able to get his battered group back to La Barquette. There he had his men dig in deep. It was at that point that Capt. Shettle appeared, requesting help at the wooden bridges over the Douve. Col. Johnson explained the situation, and told Shettle he'd have to fend for himself. The best he could promise was active patrolling between the two groups to maintain contact.

Lt. Col. Ballard had the best jump of all battalion commanders. He landed about 500 yards from a hamlet called Les Droueries, which was about that same distance from St. Côme-du-Mont, Ballard's target. All the highway bridges 2nd Battalion was supposed to destroy were on that section of highway between St. Côme-du-Mont and Carentan, three miles away.

The rest of Ballard's battalion did not fare as well as he, however. Most of them landed in swampland around Carentan, losing their equipment and weapons. Soon after landing, Ballard found a couple of sergeants, then his exec, Maj. Raymond V. Bottomly. The major had a badly twisted ankle. "Can you walk on it?" asked Col. Ballard. "No," replied the gallant major, "but I can do a damn good job of crawling."

With the help of his two sergeants, Ballard got Bottomly to a section of high ground, and told him they would make that the gathering point for 2nd Battalion men. Then Ballard set out with the sergeants, looking for men and equipment bundles. Over the next two hours, shivering men from a number of units crawled out of the swamps and gathered together. Equipment and weapons were trundled in. Just before first light, Col. Ballard felt he had enough men to make a move. He also had gathered up two machine guns, one bazooka, and a 60mm mortar. With the help of Bottomly, he organized three "Companies" of 30 men each into a makeshift battalion. Normally a company would have about 140 men. He designated them D (Dog) E (Easy) and F (Fox), in the usual line company manner, [1st Battalion companies would have been A(Able) B(Baker) and C (Charley); 3rd Battalion, G (George) H(How) and I(Item).]

Also on hand were two medics and some men from the 326th Engineers, the Screaming Eagles' demolition experts.

As Ballard was preparing to move his men out toward St. Côme-du-Mont, an incoming trooper reported seeing enemy soldiers around the farm buildings at Les Droueries. Ballard knew he'd have to clean out this hamlet before he did anything else. He couldn't possibly bypass it and leave a strong enemy force in his rear.

As dawn broke over the battlefield, Easy and Fox Companies slipped along the hedgerows, moving in to attack from different angles. Dog Company trailed behind Fox Company, as the reserve unit. The men moved cautiously along the hedgerows, getting into position. Lt. Leo Malek of Fox Company set up the mortar behind the hedgerow. Ahead of his platoon was an open pasture.

The Germans spotted the troopers then and opened fire. Malek got his mortar into action. The Germans countered with a whole battery of mortars. The troopers leaped out from behind the hedgerows and charged the farm buildings.

The German mortars caught them in the open—five men dropped, then ten, killed and wounded. The attack faded; the men ran back to the shelter of the hedgerows.

After an exchange of small arms and mortar fire, the attack resumed. Five more troopers fell. Again the two skeleton companies had to fall back. Col. Ballard realized that his undermanned unit did not have the muscle to take Les Droueries. And yet, what could he do? There were no reinforcements available. He was supposed to go on to St. Côme-du-Mont and attack the highway bridges, but to move around Les Droueries and let this strong German force be a threat to his rear was unthinkable.

While he was writhing on the horns of this terrible dilemma, Lt. Walter Wood, of the 1st Battalion of the 501st, came up to his position with twenty troopers of the 506th. Ballard decided that this fresh group of men might lead a successful new attack. He gave Wood his one bazooka, and told him to try to outflank the farm buildings with a wide swing around to the right.

Wood jumped off quickly with his group and promptly came under heavy small arms fire. Bullets clipped twigs and leaves all around him as he led his twenty men along a hedgerow on the opposite side of the road from Easy Company's position. Setting up his bazooka, Lt. Wood blasted the Germans out of the first house. When they saw the Germans fleeing, Easy Company charged forward, sent a shower of grenades through the windows of another house, followed up with small arms fire, and routed the Germans from this building.

The Germans quickly recovered and counterattacked. Under cover of a renewed mortar barrage, a platoon of the enemy made a rush for Wood's position. His men cut them down with accurate small arms fire. The troopers then tried to drive the Germans out of the rest of the buildings, but they in their turn were driven back.

So the battle swayed back and forth. Neither force could drive the other out of their stone buildings. All day and into the evening of D-Day Ballard's men and the Germans sniped and shelled each other. The casualties mounted on both sides. But nobody gave up so much as another inch.

As darkness approached, Col. Ballard sensed that this might be the propitious time to get his men out and obey Col. Johnson's order to join forces. His men were in a better position than they were earlier in the day to provide rear guard covering fire. The gathering darkness would provide additional cover. He sent a strong patrol out first toward Addeville, to seek a way around the strong German defenses, through the marshes, to the locks at La Barquette. The idea was to pick up Major Allen and his men at Addeville, and for the combined forces to fight their way through to Col. Johnson.

Hard on the heels of this patrol, half of Ballard's men moved out, carrying the wounded with them. Half an hour later the remaining force moved out. The group headed north, skirting south of Angoville-au-Plain, where a force of airborne engineers was battling units of the crack German 6th Parachute Regiment. Ballard then made a U-turn and headed south again, trying to pick his way along dry land between the marshes and the hedgerows.

The Germans met them with a wall of fire. Mortars and automatic weapons cut into them. The troopers waded into the swamp, seeking cover in the tall marsh grasses. On the other end of the swamp was an embankment and the ever-present hedgerow. From this vantage point the well-entrenched Germans poured fire into the troopers. The only way out for Ballard and his men was straight ahead.

What was left of Easy and Fox Companies stormed the hedgerow. They drove the Germans out. The next hedgerow was about 200 yards away, across an open field. Again the men charged. Lead and shrapnel reduced their ranks by another dozen troopers. But Ballard's men were in close now, lobbing grenades. The Germans countered with a shower of their own "potato mashers."

And then Col. Ballard got word over his radio that Maj. Allen had pulled out of Addeville and had joined Col. Johnson at the locks. Addeville was in enemy hands. Ballard was stuck where he was. For the moment, there was no way he could fight through to La Barquette and join the rest of the regiment.

As D-Day came to end, and the combined American-British-Canadian seaborne forces moved inland off the beaches, the field situation for the 101st was good—but it could have been a lot better. Less than half of the division was organized and in action against the enemy. Due to the scattering of the men during the night drop, most of the artillerymen of the 377th Parachute Field Artillery fought as infantry. Only one 75mm howitzer was salvaged for use. The remainder were either lost or dropped so far away they had to be abandoned.

D-Day had been a day of scattered, confused action. Due to the courage and fighting ability of the Screaming Eagles Division, individual units, fighting against tremendous odds, had managed to complete most of the missions assigned. Casualties had been heavy. But that night, Gen. Taylor and his staff went to a meeting at Culoville with Col. Sink of the 506th, secure in the knowledge that his men had met the *Wermacht,* the scourge of Europe for five years, and had shown they could beat them.

To the north, around Foucarville, the 502nd were in good shape. The exits from the beaches had been cleared on schedule. Men and armor of the 4th Division were coming through. But it was on the southern flank of the division that Gen. Taylor was to look that night. Here the Screaming Eagles were in trouble. The wooden bridges over the Douve were being held by a thread. Capt. Shettle and his small band could be swept away by one strong German counterattack. Col. Johnson's hold on the La Barquette locks wasn't much stronger. The highway and railroad bridges were still under German control. At any moment the Germans could send a whole Panzer division across those bridges and threaten the entire beachhead area.

To Gen. Taylor, the task of his division for D plus 1 was clear. Col. Sink was in the best position, with the most substantial concentration of forces. Thus it was to Col. Sink that Gen. Taylor said that night, "Get those bridges!"

Chapter Four

Early on the morning of June 7, Col. Sink began his advance. He had under him about 500 men of the 1st and 2nd Battalions, some strays from the 82nd Airborne, and a few of his own engineers and glider troops, plus an antitank unit. The advance was to take this combat team through Vierville (Vierville-sur-Mer) and Beaumont and into St. Côme-du-Mont, about a mile from the highway bridges.

The dawn of a clear day was just breaking when Lt. Col. Turner moved out on the road to Vierville with the troopers of his 1st Battalion. Men of Company A had the point. (The grim assignment of a point man was to draw enemy fire, so as to disclose enemy defensive positions.) Behind the lead battalion came the 2nd, then HQ Company, then the antitank unit, and finally the engineers, with their demolitions teams.

It didn't take long for the point men to flush out the enemy. The column was barely under way before harassing fire poured out of the houses and hedges lining the road. The troopers' advance slowed to a crawl, as yard by yard Germans fought tenaciously for the road. One by one the houses had to be cleaned out, the hedgerows flushed of snipers as hunters might flush a covey of quail.

About nine o'clock elements of the 1st Battalion reached

Vierville. The Germans were determined to hold onto the town. Furious house-to-house fighting erupted. The troopers of 1st Battalion found themselves locked in a struggle with a crack SS battalion and paratroops. Using grenades, rifles, pistols, even knives, the two sides fought a ruthless, no-prisoners-taken battle. Street by street, house by house, room by room the battle raged, squad against squad, man against man. The little town was torn apart. The wounded, the dead, and the dying littered the streets.

But by late morning the 1st Battalion secured the town. The Germans fell back. Gen. Taylor and Col. Sink moved into Vierville, and the 1st Battalion moved out again. The troopers formed up on the road that led from Vierville to Beaumont. The road was lined with ditches on either side, with steep banks rising beyond the ditches to a height of six or seven feet. Unseen by the men of 1st Battalion, Germans sneaked along the tops of these banks, then suddenly un-loosed a hurricane of automatic weapons fire. The troopers dived frantically for the ditches. Bullets slammed into them. Blindly they fired back in the direction of the unseen enemy.

The surprise attack spread confusion in the ranks of 1st Battalion. But not for long. Without waiting for orders from their officers, men sprang from the ditches—alone, or in two's and three's, they scrambled up the banks and charged head-long at the Germans, screaming and firing their weapons. Now it was the Germans who were surprised. They had ex-pected the Americans to panic, to flee to the rear. Instead, here they were, these fearsome paratroopers, counterattack-ing into blazing machine guns.

And it was the Germans who were routed.

The advance resumed. About three-quarters of a mile past Vierville the battalion paused for a breather. There the men were cheered by the arrival of six Sherman tanks of the 746th Tank Battalion. They headed for Beaumont, the tanks leading the way, machine guns spraying the hedgerows. The troopers followed behind the big tanks, crouching low to avoid the sniper fire. German mortars and 88's now opened up on the column.

Progress was slow and painful. The Germans were on both sides of the road, contesting every inch. A seesaw fight broke out around Beaumont. Company A drove into the town. A heavy German force counterattacked and drove them out. Company B was sent into the battle and drove the Germans out once again. The battalion regrouped. The tanks moved out front. In the lead tank Lt. Col. Turner himself began to call the shots, directing the machine gun and cannon fire of the tanks behind him toward the German machine gun positions. In order to see and report these German positions, Col. Turner could not play it safe and ride "hull down," with the turret sealed. He rode into battle with his head raised from an open turret, calling signals.

Just a few yards out of Beaumont a German sniper shot him in the head.

Late that afternoon Col. Sink sent ninety-four men of Company D and a platoon of light Gen. Grant tanks out of Vierville and down to Beaumont to help the beleaguered troopers there. Led by Capt. Joe F. MacMillan, the group passed through A and B Companies and proceeded to drive the Germans some half mile down the road. At 6:30 P.M. the lead Gen. Grant was working with troopers of A and D Companies, well down the road. The tank would race up and down along the ditches and hedgerows, spraying its machine gun and its 37mm cannon, while the troopers moved in behind it, picking off those Germans who broke from cover to flee the tank fire. Then, at a crossroads near St. Côme-du-Mont, an armor-piercing shell from an 88 caught the tank right through its turret. The little tank exploded and began to burn. The crew was killed instantly, the tank commander's body draped out of the open turret.

For days, while the battle raged around that crossroads, the burnt out tank and its dead crew remained in place. The crossroads became known as "Dead Man's Corner." It is still known by that name in France today.

With the tank knocked out, the forward motion of the Screaming Eagles was halted. The men dug in as a furious artillery duel broke out. The Germans were zeroed in accurately on the road, tearing it to shreds, ripping apart anything that moved on it near Dead Man's Corner. The American artillery sent out counterbattery fire from its own 75mm and 105mm howitizer battalions. The artillery observers were right up front with the men of A and D Companies, crouched in the grass atop of the road banks.

As night fell, it was clear to Capt. MacMillan that not only was he stopped cold, he was in fact too far extended. He had nothing right behind him for support. Nothing could get through, despite the fact that the American artillery had done a good job of silencing the German 88's. He moved his men back several hundred yards. Then, about midnight, Col. Sink ordered all his units to fall back onto Beaumont, and dig in for the night.

While the battle pressed on doggedly around Beaumont and the road to St. Côme-du-Mont, the other regiments of the 101st were consolidating their positions, moving forward, and trying to establish flank contact with Col. Sink and the 506th. At the same time, badly needed reinforcements were arriving over Utah Beach. These were Screaming Eagle units not committed to the airborne assault. Two battalions of the 327th Glider Regiment were in Ste. Marie-du-Mont; 3rd Battalion, by the evening of D plus 1, had made contact with the 506th troopers at Angoville. Artillery was now being provided by the self-propelled 105's of the 65th Armored Field Artillery Battalion which had come ashore on D-Day (since the 101st's own artillery was almost completely lost during the night drop).

By the night of June 7, as the 506th dug itself in around Beaumont, Gen. Taylor knew that at all costs his men had to break through St. Côme-du-Mont, secure the highway to Carentan, capture now, if he could, the crossings, and finally take Carentan itself. This mission was of the utmost urgency, because the Germans now knew what was happening along the Normandy front, and understood the importance of Carentan and the bridge crossings. There was more to it than just the control of the roadways and bridges for the passage of armor. Carentan now stood as the key to the knitting together of the American invasion forces. It sat on the left flank of the 101st, dividing the units which had landed at Utah Beach from those which had landed on Omaha Beach.

Field Marshall Rommel, back from Germany, pinpointed the town of Carentan on his situation map. He meant to hold that position and use it as the springboard for a counterattack that could split the two American army corps right back to the beaches. He sent the Order of the Day out to the *6th Parachute Regiment,* which held the town: Carentan will be defended to the last man.

The attack by the 101st on the morning of June 8 began with a rolling artillery barrage that lasted more than an hour. Some 2500 rounds of 105mm fell on the German positions. Then a three-pronged advance began behind the artillery; one directly down the road to St. Côme-du-Mont, coordinated with a double envelopment by the 501st and the 327th behind the town, to recover the ground around Dead Man's Corner yielded the night before.

By eight that morning Col. Ewell and his 3rd Battalion of the 101st had penetrated to Dead Man's Corner. He decided to push on, though the 506th, on his right flank, was stalled. But his troopers were met by heavy 88 fire from Carentan and machine gun fire from the buildings at the first bridge. As his men formed into skirmish lines to meet this fire, they were hit from behind by the German paratroopers. The battalion turned to meet this attack. Again and again the Germans charged the American lines. Each time the attack was beaten back, but each time the Germans came closer to breaking through.

During the afternoon the situation became precarious for Ewell's battalion. His men began to yield slightly under the tremendous pressure of the constant German attacks. The lines wavered. Ewell took in the situation. He moved forward, then ran to a hill overlooking the road, where some of his men were entrenched.

"Follow me!" he shouted, waving his arms. The men sprang from their positions. Ewell led them through intense enemy fire in a wide circle across the road and around the rear of an enemy-held hedgerow. Now he had outflanked the German position. He and his men poured fire down the hedgerow line. Encouraged by Ewell's courageous maneuver, three light tanks clanked forward in a direct attack on the German position. Other troopers of the 3rd now rose from concealment and followed the tanks. Caught in a brutal crossfire, the Germans retreated, leaving behind their dead and wounded. For the moment, at least, the pressure was relieved. (Col. Ewell was awarded the Silver Star for gallantry in action.)

Six times that day the Germans counterattacked 3rd Battalion. Six times they were driven off. The battalion lost 25 percent of its men killed or wounded, but it held its hard-won ground. Finally, the Germans gave up the struggle.

They withdrew from St. Côme-du-Mont, but not before blowing up the No. 2 bridge across the causeway into Carentan.

Since blowing up these bridges was part of the 101st's assignment, it seemed as though the Germans had done part of their job for them. But the situation had suddenly reversed itself. Gen. Taylor now preferred that his Screaming Eagles capture the Carentan bridges intact, for use by the advancing American forces. The Germans, however, were not stupid. They realized that their golden opportunity for a large-scale armored attack out of Carentan was lost. But it was still a vital crossroads town. Therefore, as a defensive maneuver, the bridges were best destroyed.

And yet, to the pleasant surprise of Gen. Taylor, the Germans destroyed only the second bridge. This proved to be a mixed blessing, as the men of the 101st were soon to discover.

From the new positions below St. Côme-du-Mont to the town of Carentan, the asphalt highway traversed about a mile of marsh. The road stood on a shoulder of earth, some six or seven feet above the surface of the marsh. It became a causeway over the Douve and Jourdan Rivers, which met in front of Carentan. This entire stretch of highway was wide open to small arms and artillery fire. There was no cover; it was possible for a man to dig a foxhole into the side of the embankment, but that was the limit of protection and concealment he could expect. Along this highway the 101st had to advance, perfect targets for the enemy. There was no other way.

After the capture of St. Côme-du-Mont, the troopers of the 506th established outposts all the way out to the blown bridge. From their foxholes, the men equipped with binoculars could see the Germans setting up machine gun nests in the houses on the outskirts of the town. When Col. Sink arrived at these forward outposts on the afternoon of June 9 and was apprised of the enemy movements, he decided to have a closer look. He picked out a few men to join him in a scouting patrol across the bridges. Normally colonels did not take out patrols, but Sink was an officer who did not believe in giving an order he was not prepared to carry out himself if necessary.

At the destroyed bridge, the men found an old rowboat. They piled in and rowed across the river. Not a shot was fired at them. On the other side they boldly stood up and marched across the third bridge. Suddenly enemy machine guns opened up all around them. Bullets ricocheted off the asphalt. The men dived for a ditch, then ran in a crouch back toward the rowboat. Some rowed, some swam back across the river. Miraculously, not a man was hit.

Col. Sink reported to Gen. Taylor the results of his patrol. That night Taylor ordered the 3rd Battalion of the 502nd— Lt. Col. Robert G. Cole's battalion—to advance through the 506th's positions and lead the attack on Carentan.

Gen. Taylor's plan was to envelop Carentan from three sides. After crossing the causeways, the 502nd was to swing around below Carentan to an objective called Hill 30, cutting off German retreat. At the same time, the 327th Glider Regiment would be attacking straight into Carentan itself from the left flank of the 502nd. The 501st would attack from a direction almost completely opposite from that of the 502nd, veer off at Carentan, and complete the encircling movement by meeting the 502nd at Hill 30.

At about midnight of June 9, 1st Lt. Ralph B. Gehauf volunteered to lead a reconnaissance patrol across the length of the causeway. He had been told to expect that by the time he reached Bridge No. 2, the engineers would have repaired it, and he could cross it safely. But when he reached the bridge, he found equipment piled around it, and the engineers dug in underneath. They told Gehauf that an 88 had discovered their presence and had been lobbing shells at them for the past hour, forcing them to quit work.

Gehauf found a small boat down at the stream. Making several trips, he and his ten-man squad crossed over and advanced to the fourth bridge. Here Gehauf found a strong roadblock. The Germans had built a heavy iron gate across the bridge, held in place by large concrete blocks. Heaving together, the men managed to move the gate about eighteen inches, enough so that one by one they wriggled through to the other side. They moved up another fifty yards. Just then a volley of flares lit up the sky all around them. German mortars and machine guns opened up. The men hit the ground on the side of the embankment. Gehauf sent one man back to the battalion, asking for mortars to be brought up. But the message arrived garbled. Gehauf and his men remained out on a limb in front of the bridge, drawing heavy fire. About four in the morning, with the second bridge still unrepaired, the attack by 3rd Battalion was called off. The men marched back to their jump-off point. But nobody informed Gehauf. He remained with his men, noting enemy machine gun and artillery positions for future use. Finally, sometime after five that morning, wondering what had happened to the battalion, he sent another messenger out. Contact was made with Col. Cole. Gehauf and his patrol withdrew to the other side of the causeways.

The troopers grabbed a few hours' sleep, then were wakened to prepare for a renewed attack. This time they were promised the support of substantial artillery fire. At noon on June 10 Col. Cole and Lt. Gehauf went up forward to see if the engineers had finally repaired the wrecked bridge. They had not. In resignation, the battalion commander set to work repairing it himself, with the aid of one of his company commanders and two enlisted men. Using ropes, planking, and an iron fence left behind by the Germans, the four men rigged a narrow, rickety foot bridge across the span.

By three o'clock, the work was finished. It could be crossed single file, but at least it could be crossed. Lt. Gehauf led the way across the creaking footbridge, 1st Platoon of Company G behind him, the men spaced about twenty feet apart. The 88 opened up on the troopers, then, from somewhere off to the right of the bridge, from the marsh, a sniper opened up. A couple of men from Company G crawled into the marsh after him. The next time the sniper fired, both men spotted him. They fired at him in turn. The sniper screamed, and sniped no more.

Except for the occasional 88 shell, the crossing was quiet. Col. Cole moved up and down the line of troopers, exhorting them to move up quickly, but to maintain their distance between men. They kept bunching up, and Cole feared one lucky 88 shell landing among them would wipe out an entire squad.

As the hours wore on, and the battalion moved up closer to the roadblock at bridge No. 4, the men began to hope that the easy advance meant the Germans were conceding Carentan.

But the Germans were just waiting. They waited until Lt. Gehauf and a few men had advanced past the roadblock at the fourth bridge, until most of G Company was strung out between the third and fourth bridges, and until the rest of the battalion was on the highway and moving up like ducks in a shooting gallery. Then they opened fire. Rifles cracked and machine guns rattled. Mortars and the lone 88 bracketed the causeway. The troopers hit the ground, diving for cover. Some toppled into the marsh, wounded or dead. Company G and 1st Platoon were hardest hit, drawing fire from a large farmhouse ahead of it and off its right flank.

Out in front of everybody, Lt. Gehauf was getting a good

view of the enemy gun emplacements. He called out to Sgt.
Delwin McKinney, one of his point men, that the American
counterbattery fire was dropping too far behind the German
positions. He told McKinney to get word back for the artillery to lower its range about 200 yards.

Cole's battalion was stuck fast along the causeway. Dug in
wherever they could find solid earth, the men returned the
Germans' fire. A couple of mortars were set up and began
to pepper the farmhouse area. The Germans were well
screened behind hedgerows, while the Americans were exposed along the length of the line. One by one the troopers
tried to move up and squeeze through the narrow opening in
the gate at bridge No. 4. The Germans had rifle and machine gun fire trained on the opening. Sparks flew from the
metal gate as bullets whined off it. Many of the men got
through. Others were hit at the opening. Enemy fire was
taking a terrible toll of the battalion up and down the line.

Col. Cole, who had been supervising the movement around
the second bridge, moved up front to see what was happening. All along the way he was horrified at what he saw. Company I, more exposed than the rest, was being methodically
butchered by the German sniper and machine gun fire. Even
the medics were being hit.

It seemed obvious to Col. Cole that at this rate his entire
battalion would be chewed to ribbons and would never be
able to pass through the narrow gap in the gate at that last
bridge. He crawled up to Capt. Robert L. Clements, CO of
Company G, and suggested that at dark he swim his men
across the river instead of trying to squeeze them through
the gap. Then Cole went back to the second bridge.

At dusk the battle seemed to slacken somewhat, as the
German gunners found it harder to spot their targets along
the causeway. But the respite was short-lived. Suddenly two

Stuka dive bombers appeared over the causeway. In turn, they screeched downward in their steep dives, let go anti-personnel bombs, climbed skyward, wheeled like vultures, and returned to strafe the troopers dug in along the causeway.

The Stukas just about finished off Company I. Thirty men were hit by bomb fragments and machine gun bullets. Men tumbled out of their foxholes and rolled down the embankments into the marshes. Stretcher bearers frantically ran back and forth. Only the badly wounded could be evacuated.

During the night, Col. Cole realized that Company G, in the forefront of the fighting, was too exhausted to carry out his plan. He then decided that Company H would be the point company, either swimming through or crossing over the river. Company G would follow in support. As for Company I, Col. Cole sent what was left of it back to the second bridge, as battalion reserve. This company was not in condition to advance. Of the eighty men who had started out on the causeway that afternoon, only twenty-three were left.

Around midnight, a sudden calm settled over the battlefield. Exhausted, emotionally wrung-out men fell asleep; their officers did not try to waken them. The Germans were perhaps equally spent by the furious hours of conflict. They quieted their own guns, though they still had the battalion trapped.

At three in the morning, Capt. Cecil Simmons began moving his men of Company H forward. He passed through Company G and slipped a few men through the opening in the iron gate. The men took no enemy fire. Encouraged, Simmons ordered the rest of his men through rapidly. Company G and Headquarters Company followed. By first light, Col. Cole had more than 250 men on the Carentan side of the causeway, ready to advance on Hill 30. In front of his men was the large farmhouse that had been the source of such heavy enemy fire the day before. The house was screened by hedgerows.

The men advanced slowly over the field toward the farmhouse. At point was Pvt. Albert W. Deiter. He was just five steps from the hedgerow when a tremendous volley of rifle, machine gun, and mortar fire erupted from the farmhouse area. A dozen men fell in the first volley. A machine gun burst shredded Deiter's left arm.

Col. Cole, up front with the men of Company H, dived into a ditch. Some forty yards behind him was an artillery captain, a liaison officer. Cole crawled back to him and ordered artillery fire put on the farmhouse and the hedgerows. In fifteen minutes shells began to fall on the Germans. The barrage lasted half an hour, yet it seemed to have no effect on the Germans. They continued to pour fire upon the troopers. For a moment Col. Cole considered withdrawing; then he knew there was only one way to knock the Germans out.

Across the road from him he saw his executive officer, Major John Stopka. He called to Stopka, "We're going to order smoke from the artillery and then make a bayonet charge on the house!" Stopka called back his okay. Col. Cole told the artillery captain what he wanted. Within a few minutes the artillery lay down a barrage of smoke screen shells. Col. Cole watched carefully until he felt the screen was just right, then he ordered the barrage lifted and pulled behind the house. Col. Cole passed the word to fix bayonets. Then he blew his whistle, rose from the ditch, and began running toward the farmhouse.

Only a few men followed him.

Maj. Stopka stood up and waved at the men behind him to get up and follow. A few men struggled up from the ditches and began to run forward.

Col. Cole, halfway across the field, kneeled and looked back. He was stunned. At first he felt the men had let him down. Then it occurred to him that in the noise and confusion of the battle, very few men had heard the order to charge as it had been shouted down the line. Bullets were kicking up dirt all around him as he knelt on the field. But he rose and went back down the line, talking to his men, urging them forward one by one, now and again turning and firing off his Colt .45 in the general direction of the farmhouse. "Goddamn it, I don't know what I'm shooting at," he shouted, "but I gotta keep on!"

Despite the tenseness of the moment, the men who heard him burst out laughing. It loosened them up, got them out of the ditches and off the ground and charging at the farmhouse. Col. Cole ran with them, Maj. Stopka right behind him, leading about fifty troopers. Men were dropping all around, but the charge carried over the ditches, over the hedges, up to the farmhouse. One squad branched off and ran around to the back of the house. Col. Cole stood there in the open, bullets whistling all around him, waving his men forward, directing traffic like a cop on a street corner.

Two men ran up to the front door, shot off the lock, and plunged inside. Except for the bodies of dead Germans, the house was empty. The two men dashed out the back door, and saw two Germans in the orchard, their rifles aimed. The troopers shot them dead.

The Germans had pulled back from the farmhouse under the pressure from Col. Cole's charge, and were reforming in the orchard and the hedgerows farther back. Cole's men began the job of routing them out with grenade and bayonet. Meanwhile, however, the enemy was still solidly entrenched behind the hedgerows on the opposite flank—the other side of the farmhouse, in the fields directly south of bridge No. 4. When the smoke cleared, the Germans resumed their firing on the causeway and the iron gate. It was the hard luck of the remnants of Company I to be moving up again just as the Germans ranged in with their machine guns. The last two officers of the company and one-third of the original survivors were hit squeezing through the gate.

Company I was now virtually wiped out. Leaderless, not one officer left, the men attached themselves to the nearest unit and fought on.

One of the officers who had failed to make the charge behind Col. Cole was Capt. Simmons, CO of Company H. He never heard the order. He was busy giving medical attention to several of his own wounded when Cole blew his whistle. A few seconds later a mortar exploded near him and he was knocked unconscious. When he came to, one of his sergeants told him what was happening. He rose, still dazed, and waved at his men to follow him. Though a German machine gun was firing straight at them from behind a hedgerow, Capt. Simmons and his men charged on, guns firing. More troopers fell. But they got the gun with a grenade. Another enemy strong point was knocked out.

When Simmons found a moment to tally his strength, he found he had only thirty men left of the eighty-four who'd started out with him that day. But the Germans, too, had suffered heavily.

For his heroic charge across the field, Lt. Col. Cole was later awarded the Medal of Honor, America's highest award for bravery. Unfortunately, he didn't live long enough to know about it. He was killed by a sniper in Holland three months later. The medal was awarded posthumously. Maj. Stopka was awarded the Distinguished Service Cross. He was killed at Bastogne just a few days after receiving it.

Lt. Gehauf and several others received Silver Stars.

The fight around the farmhouse slowed for a few minutes.

Col. Cole took stock of his men and the situation, and sent a runner back to Lt. Col. Cassidy with a message to bring on 1st Battalion. Cole knew that his own battalion had had it. He barely had enough men left to form a solid defense line, much less go on to complete his mission, the capture of Hill 30.

Col. Cassidy and Col. Cole got their heads together and planned their next moves. Third Battalion, or at least what was left of it, would dig in and hold the ground around the farmhouse. First Battalion would try to sustain the momentum of the attack and go all the way to Hill 30.

Company B of 1st Battalion was already in the fight, moving up through the hedgerows behind the house. But when Company A came over the causeway and across the field where Col. Cole had led the charge, the Germans caught the troopers in a tremendous barrage of mortar and 88 fire. The entire field seemed to blow up in their faces. Fifteen men were hit in the first few seconds. The rest of the company dived into ditches already overflowing with wounded or ran back to the causeway.

And so the battle raged all that day—one of the bloodiest day's fighting in the entire war. During a strange lull in the action late that morning, Company C moved up into the lines, and Cassidy's battalion was now entirely committed. What worried both battalion commanders now was that they had no reserves. If their men couldn't hold on, they would have to retreat to the other end of the causeways. This would deal a serious blow to the three-pronged attack on Carentan.

The Germans appeared to be fighting indeed to the last man, as ordered. They were being helped by the nature of the countryside around Carentan, typical of Normandy. The fields were divided into various shapes and separated by the famous Normandy hedgerows—picturesque, but now ever so deadly. Each field became in effect a completely separate battlefield, shielded from the next by the thick hedges. The troopers of the 502nd had to split up into small groups and take each field in turn, each held by a desperate enemy well entrenched behind the hedges. The artillery observers, working with Col. Cole in the farmhouse, couldn't even see where the shells were falling, so thick was the vegetation.

Often the Germans and the troopers fought on opposite sides of the same hedge, firing blindly through the vegetation, lobbing grenades through the breaks. When the troopers won a hedge, they then faced an open field, with no cover between them and the next hedge, which might be a hundred, or two hundred yards away. They would run across, firing from the hip at unseen targets, into the face of rifle, machine gun, and mortar fire. The fields were being littered with dead—American dead, German dead.

Shortly after noon the Germans asked for a truce. It was hoped that they wanted to surrender Carentan, but the hope was short-lived. The truce merely enabled both sides to remove the dead and wounded, then the awful battle resumed, one hour later. The Germans returned to the fighting with their heaviest artillery and mortar barrage of the day. American artillery returned the fire, ranging in on the hedgerows.

In the afternoon the volume of fire from the enemy increased. It was clear that a large scale counterattack was coming. The Germans intended to wipe out both battalions fighting around the farmhouse, and they didn't care how many men it might cost them. The troopers fighting around the hedgerows could hear the noise increasing as the German infantry advanced, rifles, burp guns, and machine guns firing full blast.

"They're coming." The word went up and down the line. Troopers jammed fresh clips into their rifles, laid out grenades. Boxes of ammo for the machine guns were brought up.

The farmhouse command post was no shelter from the

storm. A mortar shell wiped out Col. Cole's staff. An enlisted man standing next to him was riddled by bullets and killed.

On came the German infantry. At a crossroad, near the orchard behind the farmhouse, Staff Sgt. Harrison Summers, the D-Day hero (not yet commissioned) commanded two machine guns. With him was Pvt. Burt, who had helped him on D-Day. Two squads of enlisted men held the ground between the guns.

The German counterattack broke like a wave over the front line of troopers. They ran along the lines of the hedgerows, throwing their potato masher grenades, firing their *Schmeissers,* working the bolts of their rifles furiously. The troopers wavered, held. In some places they fired blindly into the hedgerows, shooting at sounds. In others they rose up out of their positions and met the charging Germans with bayonet and knife.

One of Summers' machine guns was knocked out, the three gunners killed. Pvt. Burt, on the other gun, just kept on firing, spraying the hedgerows and the fields, traversing his gun in an arc. He never saw a German, but later, twenty-five yards in front of his gun, bodies were found piled up behind the hedges.

Again and again the Germans attacked, fell back, and attacked again. The twenty-eight men working the machine gun positions with Summers were reduced in numbers to twelve. But not a man fell back. All along the line the ranks were thinning. And along the causeway, forward of Bridge No. 4, not a vehicle could move up under the intense fire. The wounded crawled back. Ammunition went forward from ditch to ditch, hand by hand, the wounded helping when they could.

The Germans were not much better off. As the afternoon wore on, they found their movements obstructed by the bodies of their own dead. The ditches were filled with them, the fields littered with dead and dying men who could not be removed with the renewal of the fighting. American artillery hammered their rear echelon areas, and harassed supply and reinforcement convoys.

Foot by foot, yard by yard, hedgerow by hedgerow, the Germans pressed closer to the farmhouse, advancing over the bodies of their own dead and over the bodies of troopers who died at their guns.

At the command post now, Col. Cole could hear the sounds of battle come closer and closer. Bullets zinged all around him, rattled off the slate roof, splintered the woodwork. He went up the stairs to the second floor, joined the artillery captain there. Together the two men looked out on the struggle going on all around them. It seemed to both men that the battle was all but lost. Mentally, Col. Cole began to make plans for an orderly withdrawal back along the causeway. He would need artillery smoke for a screen, just as he'd needed it for the charge that took the farmhouse.

Still, there was one last thin hope. If only he could get a sustained, strong artillery barrage in close, right on top of the German infantry, almost on top of his own positions . . .

But the radio was jammed. The artillery captain was having trouble getting back to the CP. Then suddenly, the airwaves were clear for a few moments. The artillery captain passed on Col. Cole's idea to the battery.

"If this doesn't work," the colonel said to the artillery captain, "we'll get the hell out of here right now."

In a few minutes the artillery battery changed its target coordinates. They lifted the barrage off the German rear areas and brought it crashing down among the hedgerows and onto the fields surrounding the command post. Inevitably, some of the shells exploded among the troopers of the 101st. A number of them were killed and wounded.

But this was one time the men in the line felt no resentment about casualties caused by their own artillery. They knew they had to have that fire brought down around them, or the day was lost.

For five full minutes the heavy explosives fell on the battle-ground. The barrage caught the German infantry out in the open, blasted them to pieces, tore great holes in the hedge-rows. The noise, the smoke, the choking geysers of earth, the shrieks of the wounded and the dying were appalling.

And then it grew quiet. The barrage ceased. Sporadic small arms fire could be heard much farther away now. The Germans were in retreat.

Col. Cole ran out of the farmhouse, rounded up a patrol, and went forward across the fields and through the hedge-rows. The men received no fire, but took no chances. They advanced in a line of skirmishers, spraying the fields and the hedges. They encountered nothing but dead Germans.

That evening, 2nd Battalion came up and took over. Cole and his men walked along the causeway, a road they named "Purple Heart Lane." Of the battalion that had started out on the attack that morning, only 121 men were left.

The ordeal had not been in vain. The fanatical defense and counterattack by the German *6th Parachute Regiment* was the enemy's last shot. The German commanders had decided to defend Carentan from its perimeter, not from within. When the 502nd wouldn't break, when that last desperate artillery barrage instead broke the Germans, the field com-manders conceded that Carentan was lost. The next day, elements of the 327th Gliders, the 501st, and the 506th (which had taken over for the battered 502nd) surrounded the town and broke in. What was left of the enemy sneaked out. At six o'clock on the evening of June 11, according to captured German Army records, the commandant of the

Carentan garrison reported to Seventh Army headquarters that Carentan had fallen.

Hitler was furious. He ordered a massive counterattack to start the next day, which would retake Carentan and drive the Screaming Eagles back to the beaches. The vaunted *17th SS Panzergrenadiers* was picked to lead the attack. The remnants of the *6th Parachute Regiment* were to assist.

For two days the attack went on. Fortunately, the 101st by then had been given time to reorganize its depleted forces. It also had behind it now some elements of the 2nd Armored Division, which had moved into the Carentan area, with heavy tanks and fresh infantry. Against this brick wall the *Panzergrenadiers* shattered themselves to pieces.

By the 15th of June, all was secure. The armor and the infantry pushed the Germans so far back, Carentan became a rear echelon reserve area. The Screaming Eagles put up a defense line south and southwest of the town. In Carentan itself the shops opened. Two weeks later the entire 101st was moved to a bivouac area some fifteen miles to the northwest, near Cherbourg. For the Screaming Eagles, the battle of Normandy was over. All missions accomplished.

On July 7, Gen. Taylor called a division assembly, and told his men, "You hit the ground running toward the enemy. You have proved the German soldier is no superman. You have beaten him on his own ground, and you can beat him on any ground."

The following week the 101st loaded onto LST's and sailed back to England for a rest. In their battle for Normandy, the Screaming Eagles had suffered 4,670 casualties.

PART II
HOLLAND

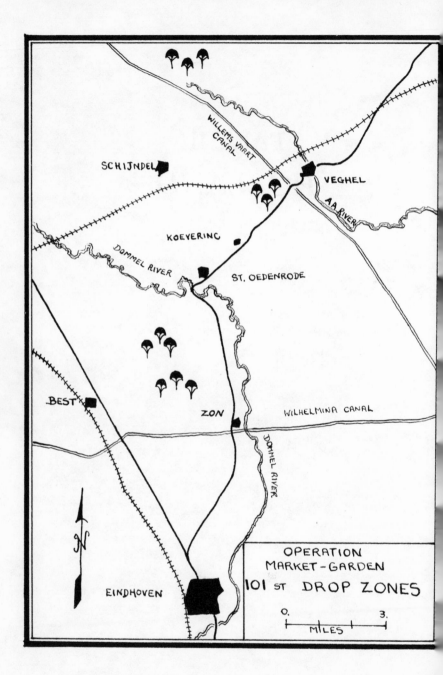

WILLEMS VAART CANAL

SCHIJNDEL

VEGHEL

AA RIVER

KOEVERING

DOMMEL RIVER

ST. OEDENRODE

BEST

ZON

WILHELMINA CANAL

DOMMEL RIVER

N

EINDHOVEN

OPERATION
MARKET-GARDEN
101 ST DROP ZONES

0.   3.
MILES

Chapter Five

During the pleasant English summer of 1944, while the Screaming Eagles were being reequipped, reorganized, and reinforced with fresh troopers, the Allied Armies were sweeping through France and Belgium. Paris was liberated in August. The Canadian First Army had cut off all the Germans along the Channel ports and almost reached the border of Holland. The British Second Army had taken Antwerp, a vital port facility for the Allies. The American First Army had pushed ahead as far as the edge of the Siegfried Line, Hitler's famous line of defense standing on the German border. General Patton and his new Third Army was racing swiftly across southeast France and had reached the Moselle River at Nancy.

That summer a new dimension was added to the Allied Armies. To the Supreme Command, the airborne operations in Normandy had proven so successful, it created the First Allied Airborne Army. The American part of this army was called the XVIII Airborne Corps, comprising the U.S. 17th, 82nd, and 101st Airborne Divisions. There were also three British airborne divisions and the 1st Polish Parachute Brigade. The American and British Troop Carrier Commands were also included. Command of the Army was given to Lt. Gen. Lewis H. Brereton, commander of the U.S. Ninth

Air Force. Command of the XVIII Corps was given to Maj. Gen. Matthew B. Ridgway, commander of the 82nd Airborne.

A number of parachute drops got to the planning stage during the summer of 1944, but the swift advance of Allied forces cancelled all of them before they could get started. The Germans were on the run, but they were a long way from being defeated. The strategy of the Allied High Command from the very beginning of Operation Overlord called for Germany itself to be invaded from the north. A thrust across the Rhine River via Holland would outflank the Siegfried Line and place the Allied Armies in a position to pour out across the plain of Westphalia, terrain suitable for the rapid movement of armor.

This was the sector under attack by the British Second Army. But in early September this Army was not capable of mounting the major attack needed for a Rhine crossing. Not without help. The British had captured Antwerp, but the port facilities were not yet operational. Their supply lines stretched over more than 200 miles of road from the Normandy ports. While Field Marshall Montgomery was confident that given time, he could drive the Germans out of Holland, strategy called for a quick breakthrough, before the Germans could build up a new line of defense along their border with Holland. As things stood, Holland's geography posed a major threat to any rapid advance by the British. The many canals and rivers crossing the country made it easy to implement delaying tactics by the retreating Germans. Bridges could be blown, roadblocks set up at vital crossings. Meanwhile, a solid defense would be building up at the border. Thus was Operation Market-Garden born.

The plan was this: On the ground (Operation Garden), the British XXX Corps, led by tanks of the Guards Armored Division, was to jump off from the Dutch-Belgian border and make a quick dash for the town of Arnhem, sixty-four miles away, on the Rhine. Ahead of them, laying out a carpet along the one highway that led across the canals and rivers to Arnhem, the First Allied Airborne Army would drop from the skies (Operation Market), "grab the bridges with thunderclap surprise," as Gen. Brereton said, and hold open the narrow corridor for the ground forces.

The one road that ran along the backbone of Holland was the key to the entire operation. This road, with its towns and bridges, was the only pathway suitable for the armor that had to cross the lowlands. The Allied High Command felt that with the bridges and other strategic points in Airborne hands, the British could race through the corridor, push past Arnhem and over the Rhine all the way to Nunspeet, on the Zuyder Zee (Ijsselmeer). This would trap all the Germans between the highway and the sea, and set the stage for a breakout into Westphalian Germany.

The schedule called for the XXX Corps to reach Arnhem within forty-eight hours, because the Airborne troops, dropping without tanks, artillery, or opportunity for resupply, could not hold out longer than that against the inevitable German counterattacks. The British First Airborne was to drop at Arnhem. South of that, where the road crossed the Waal at Nijmegen and the Maas at Grave, the 82nd would drop.

The task of the 101st was to seize a sixteen-mile stretch of road that began behind the German front line at Eindhoven and ran north through the towns of Son, St. Oedenrode, and Veghel (Vechel).

Together, the Allied Airborne forces glider and parachute numbered some 35,000 men.

The mission assigned the Screaming Eagles was especially crucial. The Guards Division was scheduled to reach them first. If the Eagles failed to open the corridor, then anything the other divisions did farther north was useless—the drive would fail at its start. Further, even after the Guards passed through, the Eagles were responsible for the security of their section of road. There would be Germans on both sides of the road trying to cut it, and sixteen miles of road was too much for one division to hold completely.

It was soon to be called "Hell's Highway" by the troopers of the 101st.

Specifically, the Screaming Eagles were to seize the rail and highway bridges over the Aa River and the Zuid Willems Vaart Canal, near Veghel; the highway bridges over the Dommel River at St. Oedenrode; and the bridges over the Wilhelmina Canal near Son; and over the Dommel River again where it ran through Eindhoven. All of these major towns were to be held; Eindhoven was the first along the line of the Guards' advance.

Gen. Taylor realized that all he could really do along that sixteen-mile corridor was hold the bridges and key towns, and keep contact between those points by means of strong patrols. Actually, the entire operation was like a long chain, with weak links all the way along the sixty-four miles of road. If at any time the Germans were able to break those weak links, the operation faced disaster.

The Allied High Command was counting on the element of surprise to bring off the operation—surprise, and intelligence reports which said that the German troops in the area were ill-organized and in some cases rear-echelon outfits which would put up little resistance in a real fight.

These intelligence reports were in a large measure correct—in a large measure, but not completely correct. There was also the danger that the operation would bite off more than it could chew; capturing and holding sixty-four miles of road behind enemy lines was at best a risky proposition. Indeed the general optimism prevailing at Allied Headquarters was by no means unanimous. One doubter was Maj. Brian Urquhart, a British Intelligence specialist. He felt his chiefs were counting too much on the weakness of German opposition. Eventually he voiced one too many negative opinions and was quietly eased out of the planning operations.

But Lt. Gen. Frederick Browning, commander of the British 1st Airborne, also had reservations. Part of his mission was the capturing of the fifth major bridge along the corridor—the bridge at Arnhem. During one of the final briefings before the assault, he said to Field Marshall Montgomery (as recalled by Maj. Gen. Roy E. Urquhart in his memoirs), "Sir, I think we might be going a bridge too far."

Nevertheless, Operation Market-Garden was set for Sunday, the 17th of September. Ten A.M. was lift-off time for some 5000 transports, bombers, and fighters, and 2500 gliders of the Airborne Army. The drop would begin at 1:30 P.M. One hour later, behind an artillery barrage and under an umbrella of fighter-bombers, Lt. Col. Joe Vandeleur's Irish Guards would launch their attack up "Hell's Highway."

The decision to make this a daylight jump had been a bold one. It was based upon two factors: the confusion and dispersement of the paratroops following the Normandy night drop, and the Allied superiority in the air. In addition, recalling the painful experiences of Normandy, Gen. Taylor insisted on a concentrated drop. Both the 502nd and 506th would drop northwest of the town of Son; the same area would be used later for glider landings.

The job assigned the 502nd was the guarding of the landing zone area, the capturing of the road bridge at St. Oedenrode, the defense of Son itself, and the support of the 506th in its attack on Eindhoven.

The 506th was to take the Wilhelmina Canal bridge at Son, then turn south and capture Eindhoven with its four highway bridges over the Dommel.

The 501st, given the northernmost drop zone to itself, had the job of capturing the highway and railroad bridges over the Aa River and the Zuid Willems Vaart Canal at Veghel.

Gen. Taylor also gave one small extra mission to the 502nd. It was to seize the road and railroad bridges at Best, to the westward of the regimental area. This was not part of the original combat zone assigned to the 101st; however, looking over the operations maps, Gen. Taylor thought it would be a good idea to help secure the flank via Best. It appeared to be a routine job and Taylor thought one platoon ought to be enough—one platoon out of Col. Cole's 3rd Battalion of the 502nd. But Cole thought he'd need a whole company; he requested and got permission to send Company H to secure Best.

What an eventful and fateful mission this supposedly routine task turned out to be.

The gamble of a daylight drop paid off. As the C-47's winged in over the Channel, not a German fighter came near them. Near the drop zones, the flak began to thicken. But this was not Normandy. The pilots of Troop Carrier Command had learned a bitter lesson well. After Normandy they had been reprimanded by Gen. Eisenhower for their costly mistakes. This time there was no evasive action to avoid the flak, no breaking of formation. Even as their planes burst into flames, pilots held on course for those vital seconds necessary for an accurate jump. Entire battalions came down together, landed close to their equipment, and were organized and operating in less than an hour. It was a "parade ground" jump.

The gliders that came in an hour later were not so lucky, seventeen of the seventy never reaching the drop zone.

To the townspeople of Veghel, awaiting their liberation from the Nazis, the sight of a whole regiment of parachutists descending around them must have filled their hearts with joy. Their town was a target of the 501st, commanded by Col. Howard "Skeets" Johnson.

The battalions dropped in a neat pattern, 2nd and 3rd together, 1st some three miles away, closer to its assignment, the river bridges. Within the hour, 2nd and 3rd had taken the town of Eerde without opposition, and sent a detachment out to put a roadblock across the Veghel-St. Oedenrode highway. With 3rd Battalion protecting its rear, 2nd Battalion advanced on Veghel. Company E went for the railroad bridge over the canal. Companies D and F and HQ Company headed down the road. They encountered nothing more serious than scattered rifle fire and the occasional machine gun burst. All the bridges were taken. Then scouts of the 2nd Battalion went on into Veghel itself. There they ran into scouts of 1st Battalion. A few die-hard Germans put up a brief fight but were quickly subdued. Fifty prisoners were taken.

The citizens of Veghel came out of their houses and swarmed through the streets, shouting and crying with joy. They offered the troopers food and drink, chattering away in broken English. For a time the war was forgotten, and the troopers found it difficult to set up defense positions in the town against German counterattacks. Finally, good sense prevailed. The Dutch returned to their homes and let the troopers carry on with their preparations.

Meanwhile, 1st Battalion found itself well organized around the drop zone, though some three miles from the target area. Quickly Lt. Col. Harry Kinnard, the battalion commander, prepared to move out on his assignment. Dutch civilians who met him at the drop zone told him he was near Kameren, astride the main road. Kinnard sent his point platoon out. These men ran into a few German staff cars along the way and at once captured the surprised occupants. Other troopers commandeered trucks, cars, and even bicycles, and sped toward the bridges. In short order the Aa River railroad bridge was seized. Kinnard then sent his scouts out toward Veghel, where they encountered the 2nd Battalion scouts and helped clear Veghel of the enemy.

For the 501st, the whole thing had been a piece of cake. The other two regiments of the 101st were not so fortunate.

Col. Sink and the 506th enjoyed a picture drop near Son. Rapidly, the regiment got itself organized and ready to move out. Minutes counted. Even as the first troopers landed, the tankers of the Irish Guards were launching their attack along the highway to Eindhoven. The first thing the 506th had to do was seize and secure the main bridge and two smaller bridges over the Wilhelmina Canal at the town of Son. The plan was to have 1st Battalion hit the bridges from the flank, while 2nd and 3rd Battalions advanced straight down the highway, through Son and south to Eindhoven, opening the way for the Guards. Gen. Taylor decided to accompany 1st Battalion, commanded, since Col. Turner's death, by Maj. James LaPrade.

All went well for the battalion until it reached the vicinity of the canal. Then a battery of 88's opened up on it. Company A, on the point, took the brunt of the fire. Several men were hit. One of the wounded was company commander Melvin C. Davis, hit by a bullet. As he was lying in a field, receiving first aid, he was hit again. He then uttered one of the war's memorable remarks. "You better hurry up, medics," he said. "They're gaining on you."

After a furious fire fight, the 88's were knocked out. The Germans fled. The battalion continued its advance, now led by Company B.

Meanwhile, 2nd Battalion was leading the rest of the regiment down the main road. At the outskirts of Son this battalion too came under 88 fire. It appeared to be just one gun, covering the road. While the battalion halted, a platoon dashed around the flank, through a group of outbuildings, and got within fifty yards of the big gun. With one shot from his bazooka, Pvt. Thomas G. Lindsey knocked out the gun with a direct hit on the elevating mechanism. One German was killed. The other six crew members fled toward the bridge. Sgt. John F. Rice of Company D killed them all with his submachine gun.

The battalion went on, wondering what had happened to the men of 1st Battalion, who should have been at the bridge by then. These troopers had no way of knowing that 1st Battalion had been delayed by an entire battery of 88's. A few minutes later, the first scouts from 1st Battalion appeared, linking both units. They were now about 150 yards from the bridge, approaching it from two angles, exchanging small arms fire with Germans in houses on the other side of the canal.

Suddenly, with a tremendous roar, the bridge went up. Debris showered down upon the stunned troopers. Col. Sink ran forward and saw that except for the center pillar, the bridge was effectively destroyed. Just then a runner came up with more bad news. The two smaller bridges had also been blown, apparently several days earlier.

Col. Sink was not entirely unprepared for this problem. He had with him a platoon of Airborne Engineers. While the troopers scrounged some small boats, crossed the canal, and began cleaning the enemy out of the houses on the other side, the engineers went to work. In short order they improvised a footbridge. However, the bridge could support just a few men at a time. It was now late afternoon. The regiment's schedule called for it to take Eindhoven and join with the Guards at 8 P.M.; obviously out of the question under the circumstances. It would take hours for the regiment to cross the little foot bridge.

That night, Col. Sink had his men take up defensive positions about a mile south of the canal. The march on Eindhoven would have to wait until morning. The colonel went to sleep in his foxhole that night afraid that his failure to secure the bridges intact and reach Eindhoven might have doomed the entire operation. As it turned out, however, the Guards ran into very heavy opposition and were themselves stalled halfway to Eindhoven. The two units would have to try again on D plus 1.

Gen. Taylor jumped with 1st Battalion of the 502nd. He set up his division Command Post, while the battalions formed around him and prepared to move on their objectives. Lt. Col. Pat Cassidy and his 1st Battalion were to take St. Oedenrode; 2nd Battalion was to remain in reserve along with the greater part of 3rd Battalion, north of Son. Company H of 3rd Battalion was sent on to take the town of Best.

St. Oedenrode was easy. For a short time B and C Companies were pinned down by small arms fire, but swift counterattacks routed the Germans. Twenty were killed and fifty-eight captured.

The experience of Company H was something else again. This "routine mission" to secure the town of Best and guard the regimental flank, originally scheduled as a platoon action, then a company task, was soon to engage an entire battalion, then two battalions, then half a division plus a squadron of British tanks.

Hard luck hit Capt. Robert E. Jones, Company H commander, from the start. He chose a route that should have brought him out on the Eindhoven-Boxtel Highway, about half a mile from Best. But going through the woods he lost sight of his church steeple landmark and came out on the highway just 400 yards from the Best crossroads. Immediately he came under enemy fire. Company H tried to force the enemy back and take the crossroads; in the counterattack it became widely dispersed. Meanwhile, 12 trucks filled with German troops arrived to take part in the skirmish. Capt. Jones reformed his lines, but then Col. Cole radioed him to get his engineer platoon, his own 2nd Platoon, and his light machine guns right down to the railroad bridges. Without these units, the captain realized his position near the crossroads would become untenable; he therefore pulled his whole company back into the protection of the woods.

Once he'd established a new defensive position there, Capt. Jones ordered Lt. Edward L. Wierzbowski to take his 2nd Platoon and the engineer platoon, and head south for the bridges. The lieutenant gamely took off, sorely under strength. During the brief battle near the crossroads he had lost a dozen men from his platoon. Missing were his platoon leader, a squad of engineers, and his entire machine gun section.

During the next forty hours, this little band of troopers was to write an epic chapter in the history of the 101st. What the lieutenant could not know, what his company commander could not know, what Gen. Taylor and the Allied Command did not know, due to faulty intelligence, was that the German 59th Infantry Division plus a considerable amount of artillery was still very much alive and kicking right in the neighborhood. Instead of being lightly held, as reported, the town of Best held upwards of a thousand enemy troops.

As the sun began sinking, but while light still filtered through the woods, Lt. Wierzbowski led his men through a plantation of pine trees. The Germans had cut fire breaks through these trees, open lanes to give machine guns clear fields of fire. As soon as the troopers began to cross the first lane, the German guns began to rattle.

The lieutenant was in no position to sacrifice men in a direct attack on machine gun nests. He had his men swing around to the right and cross any fire lanes in short rushes. Though he preferred arriving at the bridges while there was still light, he saw no point in arriving there with the unit cut still further to pieces. As a result, by the time the group got to the edge of the woods, it was dark, and it was raining.

Ahead of the troopers now was open ground. Pvt. Joe E. Mann, the lead scout, crawled out ahead of the others, skirted a small marsh, and finally came out on the dike bounding the canal. The men followed him over the dike, down to the bank of the canal toward the bridge. In the darkness, they felt their way until they came to a spot where two large derricks and a loading zone blocked their way. It was now about 9 P.M., and Lt. Wierzbowski figured they still had about 500 yards to go to reach the bridge.

Willing to gamble, Wierzbowski sent Mann on up ahead, while he led the rest of the men along a wet and slippery catwalk suspended around the derricks, out over the canal. He knew that if the Germans sent up one flare while he and his men were thus exposed, it was the end of all of them. But their luck held—at least for the moment.

On the other bank, Wierzbowski crawled up to the point, joining Mann. Not yet seeing the bridge, the two men crawled on. And they went too far. By coincidence, Wierzbowski and Mann had slipped through the German sentry point just as the guards were being changed around the bridge. When the new guard came on, the two men found they were stuck inside his beat. They couldn't kill him, because periodically he shouted and fired his gun in signal to the guard on the other side of the bridge. Neither could they slip back past him without the risk of being seen. Thus they stayed put, the lieutenant and the private, wondering what to do.

Half an hour later, the men they had left behind suddenly came under attack. A volley of grenades began the surprise assault. Some of the men jumped up, and were promptly cut down by machine gun and rifle fire. But the attack provided the diversion needed by Wierzbowski and Mann. They made a run for it and got back to the platoon. Then mortar and artillery fire began to fall around them. Wierzbowski ordered his men to fall back sixty yards and dig in. He then took a head count: he had fifteen men and three officers left. All were low on ammunition.

At 3 A.M. the enemy firing stopped. But the rain continued to pelt down.

Capt. Jones, meantime, wondering why he hadn't heard from Wierzbowski, sent patrols out to find him. They couldn't get through the German fire in the pine woods. Then Jones sent in the entire 3rd Platoon. It fared no better. During the night, while Wierzbowski and his men huddled near the canal, Company H took a pasting from the German guns, losing thirty-nine men killed and wounded.

As soon as the first reports from Capt. Jones got back to Regimental HQ, it was realized that the enemy strength at Best had been badly underestimated. So the rest of 3rd Battalion was sent forward to help. It got within a mile of the town when heavy mortar and artillery fire blocked further advance. The men dug in for the night. Patrols were unable to get through to Company H, although radio contact was maintained.

Thus, as the first day of battle in Holland came to an

end, the 101st could report most of its objectives gained. Except for the capture of Eindhoven, all towns and bridges had been taken. The unexpected enemy resistance at Best was proving to be a thorn in the side of the Division, but this was considered to be a secondary objective, not part of the initial mission.

All in all, it could have been much worse—but the worst was yet to come.

Farther north along the corridor, the American 82nd Airborne and the British 1st Airborne were having their own serious problems with a determined enemy. The entire operation was behind schedule.

On D plus 1 the task for the Screaming Eagles was abundantly clear: they had to capture Best and Eindhoven and open up the rest of the corridor for the tanks of the Guards.

Chapter Six

At first light of the new day Lt. Wierzbowski and his men got their first clear view of the bridge they had been sent to take. It was a tantalizing sight—so near, yet so far. The bridge was not much, as bridges go, a one-span concrete structure, something over a hundred feet long. Still, it was a bridge that could be used to good advantage, especially with the Son bridge out.

To Wierzbowski, it appeared that the north end of the bridge had been left unguarded. But south of the bridge he spied a barracks, with dug-in positions all around it. These positions were filled with enemy soldiers. There was another group of Germans on the other side of the road, about eighty yards away. Anytime one of the troopers showed himself a bit too much, the Germans opened up from both sides.

Early that morning the men saw a group of Germans straying toward them from the trees along the north bank of the canal, stragglers from the 2nd Battalion attack. The troopers held their fire until the Germans got to within fifty yards. Then they let loose and mowed them down, killing about thirty-five.

About 10 A.M., the watching men saw a German soldier and a civilian move up to the far side of the bridge. They stood around for about twenty minutes, apparently doing nothing but chatting. The men wanted to take a shot at the German, but, figuring the civilian was Dutch, they held back lest a stray bullet harm a friendly civilian.

An hour later there came a terrific explosion. The span shook and lifted. Concrete and steel debris flew high in the air and rained down on the troops in their foxholes. It became clear then that the German and the civilian had been more than just chatting; they had obviously set a time fuse to a previously planted demolition. So now the Best bridge was gone, but Wierzbowski had no way to relate this information to Regiment. The staff at headquarters thought this prize could still be won.

Nevertheless, Wierzbowski and his men felt they had been sent out to do a job, and they would stay on and do the best they could. Mann and another trooper, an engineer named Northrup, went forward with a bazooka, under covering fire from the rest. A hundred yards out they spotted an 88 ammunition dump. Mann destroyed it with the bazooka. Then the two men stayed out near the dump, pot-shotting stray Germans. In the next hour they killed six. But then the Germans zeroed in on them. Mann was hit twice by rifle bullets. Northrup knocked out an 88 gun with the bazooka, then the two men ran back to their original positions. Though wounded, Mann picked up a rifle and continued the fight until an aid man came up and bandaged him.

In midafternoon the Germans mounted an attack, but were driven off. To get a better view of the retreating enemy, Lt. James Watson of the engineers crawled out in front of his foxhole. He was hit at once in the groin. Medic James Orvac went out after him, followed by Wierzbowski. The lieutenant was in terrible pain. He thought his private parts had been shot off. He begged Lt. Wierzbowski to take his .45 pistol and kill him. Instead Wierzbowski dragged him back and put him with the rest of the wounded. Watson later died.

Now the German fire increased in strength. Mortars and artillery were added to the rifle and machine gun fire. Northrup was hit in the spine and killed. Two more bullets bored into Mann. They bandaged him again and put his arms in slings. Wierzbowski ordered him back with the other wounded, to a safer foxhole. Mann asked to stay with the rest; his request was granted.

By this time the medical supplies were exhausted. Lt. Otto J. Laier and Staff Sgt. Thomas A. Betrus volunteered to try to break through for aid. They sneaked away. A few minutes later Betrus came back, wounded. They had been ambushed. Laier had been wounded too, and captured.

All during this grim struggle the beleaguered men could hear the sounds of heavy firing coming from the woods where the rest of their battalion was in action. They felt confident they would be relieved. But as the day wore on and the situation grew more serious, they began to lose hope; indeed, unknown to them, Regiment had already given them up for lost.

Then their hopes were suddenly revived. From out of nowhere a British armored car and a reconnaissance car appeared on the other side of the canal. The Germans turned their fire on them. The cars pulled around a corner of a building and began blazing away with all their machine guns. The Germans dug in around the barracks area got out and ran.

Cpl. Daniel L. Corman dashed down to the canal bank, found a small boat, and rowed across to the cars. He came back with a medical aid kit. Wierzbowski shouted across to the British asking them to call Division HQ on their radio and explain the need for help. The British couldn't get through. Then Wierzbowski got up and began to move his men down the bank, planning to row them across the canal, where they would enjoy the protection of the two scout cars.

Only the British weren't planning on hanging around. "Stay where you are!" shouted the British commander. "I'm sure that help will be here soon!"

Three troopers then prowled around near the derricks and came back with three German medics and a wounded German officer. He told the medics to get to work on his men, which they did.

Again things seemed to take a turn for the better when a patrol from Company E got through to them early that evening. The men soon left, promising to take back word of the destruction of the bridge and the plight of the group. But somehow the patrol report arrived back at Battalion distorted. It told only of the destruction of the bridge.

Later an entire platoon from Company D, 2nd Battalion, appeared on the scene. Lt. Nicholas D. Mottola, the platoon leader, decided it was more prudent to remain with the Wierzbowski group than to try to return to Battalion in the dark. The lines were reorganized for the night, with the Mottola group holding down one flank. Feeling a bit more secure now, the exhausted survivors from Wierzbowski's group fell asleep. The British scout cars, learning of the new platoon's arrival and concluding that relief had arrived, slipped away from the far bank.

In the middle of the night Mottola's group was hit hard by a German attack. The platoon fell back, became almost completely dispersed, and eventually took two days to rejoin its battalion.

Lt. Wierzbowski woke up the next morning and found his group was all alone.

And there, coming through the morning mist not twenty feet away from him, was a group of Germans. He yelled.

Sgt. Betrus threw a grenade. Some of the other men woke up fast and threw grenades. Rifle fire was exchanged. Pvt. Mann, four times wounded, grabbed a rifle and took snap shots as best he could. Another shower of grenades came hurtling over. Two rolled into the foxhole among the wounded. Betrus threw one out. Another trooper threw out the second.

More grenades came. One went wild. Then one of the potato mashers hit the machine gun and exploded right into Pvt. Vincent Laino's face. It blew out his left eye, blinded the other, and made a bloody pulp of his face.

A bullet hit Pvt. Lawrence J. Koller in the head and killed him. Another grenade came in, hit Laino on the knee, and bounced away. Still blinded, he managed to grope for it, find it, and toss it back just a split second before it exploded.

The next grenade came toward Mann. He was sitting against the back of the large foxhole—a foxhole containing six other men—and he saw the grenade land. He hadn't the strength left or the time to throw it out. Yelling, "Grenade!" he threw himself backward and took the full force of the explosion with his own body. It blew his back apart.

Mann said quietly to Wierzbowski, "My back's gone." A minute or so later he died—the bravest man, his comrades said, that they had ever known.

Pvt. Joe E. Mann was later awarded, posthumously, the Medal of Honor.

The Germans kept coming. The troopers were out of ammunition. Only three men were left unwounded. Further struggle was pointless. Lt. Wierzbowski and his group surrendered.

Many men of the 502nd speak with greater pride of the events at Best than of any other single action in the history of the regiment. Even though unsuccessful, the attack exemplified the heights of combat discipline to which paratroopers of the Screaming Eagles Division were trained.

At first light of D plus 1, Col. Cole had succeeded in making physical contact with Company H. But during the night the Germans obviously had been reinforced. Quickly they drove 3rd Battalion even farther back into the woods. Col. Cole knew then that taking Best and its bridges was too big a job for his battalion. At Regiment, Col. John H. Michaelis, the CO, was reaching the same conclusion. At once he ordered Lt. Col. Steve A. Chappuis to take his 2nd Battalion and join the battle. Chappuis was to advance on the right of 3rd Battalion, establish contact on the flank, pivot on it, and attack on through Best down to the bridges.

The battalion advanced across the fields, Company D on the left, E and F to its right. Company D reached 2nd Battalion's right flank, and the 3rd Battalion made its pivot.

It looked for all the world like a parade ground maneuver. The company commanders led the way. The platoon leaders urged on the men. The squad leaders were out front, leading. From left to right, in lines of skirmishers, the battalion went forward across the fields. Piles of hay were in the fields. In groups of two's and three's the men went from haystack to haystack, in perfect order, with perfect discipline.

But this was not a parade ground maneuver. On the other end of the fields the Germans were waiting. They waited and waited, and then opened up with artillery, mortars, rifles, and machine guns. The heavy staccato of the German guns was answered in part by the rifles and Tommy guns of the troopers. Their mortars answered the German mortars —but there was nothing to counter the deadly shelling of the 88's. The 101st had no artillery. None was dropped with them; none was coming in that day with the gliders. It was thought none would be necessary; this was supposed to have been a forty-eight hour action, in and out, hold till the armor busts through, and then more armor would expand the corridor and take over.

It wasn't happening that way. The hayfields became a slaughterhouse. German machine gun fire cut through the haystacks, setting some on fire, killing and wounding the men sheltering behind them as though they were made of concrete. Shrapnel flew across the open spaces like thousands of red hot scythes. Troopers were cut down by the dozen. Eight officers lay dead or wounded. Casualties were running more than 20 percent. It couldn't go on. The battalion could not continue to take such losses and exist. But the troopers stayed in there, moving forward, the lines unwavering, until Col. Chappuis stopped it. He pulled his men back.

The Germans then shifted their fire to Cole's 3rd Battalion. Small enemy units began to infiltrate 3rd's positions. Cole called for some air support. In a few minutes a flight of P-47's zoomed in low over the trees, and in error began strafing Cole's own men. Quickly Cole went out in front of his lines with a few of his troopers and began laying out orange identification panels.

The P-47's came back for another pass, got the message, and began strafing the German positions. The enemy fire slackened. Col. Cole rose from a foxhole and walked forward, perhaps to adjust one of the panels, perhaps to get a better look at the strafing job being done by the P-47's. No one will ever know. A sniper's bullet from a house a hundred yards away hit him in the head, killing him instantly.

As Cole fell, a lone German ran from the house. One of the battalion machine guns cut him down. The men figured this was the sniper who had shot Col. Cole. They couldn't be sure, but it comforted them to tell each other that they'd got the German who killed their colonel.

Lt. Watson, who was near Cole when he was hit, could not bring himself to utter the phrase, "Cole is dead." Instead, he sent second-in-command Maj. John F. Stopka this message: "You are in command of the battalion." For the next hour or so Maj. Stopka thought this was just a temporary measure.

Enemy artillery fire continued to harass 3rd Battalion all through the day, while the 2nd reorganized for another push. Heroic actions by individual troopers were numerous during the hours of fierce fighting.

Pvt. Robert S. Doiel, platoon scout, at one point found himself far out in front of his comrades, within a hundred yards of the enemy lines. A rifle bullet hit him in the shoulder. He fired back and killed two of the enemy. His one-man attack brought him the attention of some nineteen Germans in a ditch to his immediate front. A small arms duel began. While Doiel shot it out with the nineteen Germans, two other troopers took advantage of the situation to crawl out to the flank and shoot at the Germans from there. Seeing the Germans now caught in a crossfire, Doiel ran forward and ordered them to surrender. Instead the Germans shot at him, wounding him again, knocking his weapon from his hands. Doiel picked up a fallen pistol and fired back. Fifteen Germans put up their hands and yelled "Kamerad!"

Doiel got his wounds bandaged by his buddies and headed back with them to the platoon with the prisoners. A mortar burst caught them and Doiel was wounded a third time. He survived, got the prisoners back, and was awarded the Silver Star.

Pvt. George R. Tobinas was another who won a Silver Star that day. During the heavy fighting, Tobinas spotted a badly wounded officer far out in front of the lines. Although himself wounded in the ankle and arm, Tobinas was determined to rescue the officer. Shouting to his buddies to hold their fire, he crawled out to the wounded man. The Germans tried to get him with rifles and machine guns.

Every few minutes Tobinas had to stop and take cover from the enemy fire, or rest because of the pain of his wounds.

He reached the wounded officer at last, lifted him to his shoulder, and carried him to safety through a hail of German bullets.

There was Pvt. William Podulski, who ran across an open field into the fire of the enemy to destroy with grenades, singlehanded, an enemy mortar position. Cut down by a machine gun halfway to his target, Podulski crawled the rest of the way, but got the job done.

Pvt. Frank Kessler lay out on his company flank, all by himself, for eight hours that day, fighting off the enemy while directing machine gun fire from his observation post.

Both troopers won Silver Stars. Both were later killed in action.

At about five o'clock on that afternoon of D plus 1, Col. Chappuis moved 2nd Battalion through 3rd's positions in another attempt at reaching the Best bridges. Nobody as yet knew that the main bridge had been blown, or knew the fate of Wierzbowski and his men. Chappuis got little more than half a mile before a heavy barrage from the German 88's stopped the battalion. That was it for the 502nd on D plus 1. The battalions dug in for the night.

Farther north, at Veghel, the 501st spent the day beating off German counterattacks, holding on to their perimeter defense of the town. To the south, the 506th marched on Eindhoven. Early on the morning of D plus 1, Col. Sink called a meeting of his battalion commanders. "If you see any Germans just let them filter through you and I guess the Ducks will take care of them," he said. (Division nickname for the 502nd was the Ducks. The 501st were the Geronimos; the 506th, after its commander, the Sinks.)

"We have got to get to Eindhoven this morning," Col. Sink

went on, "and we can't waste any time killing Germans."

Leaving behind Company A and an engineer platoon to guard the bridge at Son, the rest of the regiment set out, 3rd Battalion leading. Within half a mile H and I Companies, out in front, took heavy machine gun fire. The two companies attacked and eliminated the German strong points. Slowly the advance continued, taking harassing fire, stopping to knock out the little groups of Germans slowing them, and then resuming the march. Then, at Eindhoven, a major city of 100,000, the battalion began getting direct fire down the main street from two 88's. Enemy mortars also shelled them. The battalion came to a complete stop.

Capt. John W. Kiley, battalion Intelligence officer, rose from the protection of a ditch and took a few tentative steps forward. A sniper killed him. Troopers pointed out the sniper's position—in a church tower. Someone got off a bazooka round. A direct hit on the tower silenced the sniper.

Col. Sink came forward. He decided that to attempt to force a direct attack down the road with 3rd Battalion would cause heavy losses. Instead he ordered a flanking movement by 2nd Battalion around to the left and down an adjoining road. Company F would attack the Germans holding up 3rd Battalion, while the other two companies moved toward the center of town.

Company F slipped through the cobbled streets, beneath shuttered windows, into Eindhoven. At the corner of Pastorie Straat and Klooster Dreef they ran into the battalion executive officer, Capt. Charles G. Shettle, who told platoon commander Lt. Russell Hall to have his men clear out the 88 battery. With him Shettle had a Dutch civilian who said he would lead the men to the battery location.

The platoon advanced quietly through Klooster Dreef, the men strung out on both sides of the street. Up front Lt. Hall placed his rifle grenadiers and his Tommy gunners. At the

corner of Run Straat, the Dutchman told them (in English)
that the gun was just around a bend in the street. Hall took
a peek, grasped the layout, and sent his men to the attack.
The block which lay between him and the 88 was triangular
in shape, with Dutch houses on all three sides. The 2nd
squad under Lt. Robert Pardue took the left side of the
block—Woenselsche Straat. Hall himself took 1st Squad in
a maneuver that would lead them between the houses of
Klooster Dreef and out the other end near the gun. The 3rd
Squad remained in the center of the block, in reserve, with
a mortar.

As the two assault squads moved into position, all was
quiet. Not a shot was fired at them. The enemy seemed to
have no idea they were in the town. In fact Sgt. George
Taylor of 1st Squad saw a German soldier walking calmly
down Klooster Dreef. Martin took a shot at him, but missed.
The soldier fled. Then Lt. Hall, along with three other men,
moving between buildings, saw a Dutch woman in a second
story window waving to them. She held up three fingers and
pointed down the street. The men stopped. Three German
soldiers then passed by, walking towards the direction of the
gun. Lt. Hall jumped out behind them. "Hold it!" he
shouted. The Germans surrendered without a fight.

From the other side of the street now, two Dutchmen
motioned the squad on toward the Woenselsche intersection,
near the church, indicating that the gun was right there.
Staff Sgt. John H. Taylor stepped out into the street and saw
the 88 at the crossroads, about 150 yards away. The Germans
saw him at the same time. Six Germans ran toward the gun.
Taylor stood at the curb and fired a full clip from his Ml.
Two of the Germans dropped. Then Taylor's gun jammed.
He ran behind a building to clear the clip and reload.

While he was thus occupied, the Germans got the 88 into
action. The first shot knocked a corner off the building about

twenty feet above Taylor's head. Taylor, with rifle grenadier Robert W. Sherwood behind him, pulled farther back behind the house for better protection. The gun fired two more rounds, knocking large chunks out of the building. It seemed to the troopers that using an 88 to try to kill two men was rather extravagant of the Germans. But if it was a duel the enemy wanted . . .

Sherwood popped out and fired two grenades at the gun. The second grenade landed just five yards behind it. At that same moment grenadier Homer Smith fired two grenades. His second was a direct hit. Sherwood yelled over to him, "We got 'em!"

Sherwood and Taylor ran across the street and met with Sgt. Frank Griffin, the mortar man. From that vantage point, some sixty-five yards from the gun, they could get a better view. And they realized then that though the grenades had hit some of the crew and driven them from the gun, the 88 itself was probably still operative. Griffin set up his mortar. A German officer approached the 88 cautiously. Taylor drew a bead on him. The first mortar round landed about fifteen yards from the gun. The German officer turned and ran toward a house. Taylor squeezed the trigger and shot him in the leg. The German went down, got up again, and ran into the house.

Griffin's second round landed squarely on the 88, knocking it out. Then Sherwood fired a grenade into the house where the officer had taken shelter. The grenade exploded inside, wounding ten Germans.

There was a second 88 nearby, however. When the first gun was knocked out, this second one opened up on the troopers. Smith fired three grenades at it, missing. But the German crew didn't wait around for a direct hit. They blew the breech of the gun, making it useless, then made a run for it. Six men from 2nd Squad moved fast across Klooster Dreef and Kaak Straat and waited behind some houses. Into their trap ran fourteen Germans from the 88 crew. The troopers fired. The Germans dropped to the ground in a beet field. The troopers yelled for them to come out and surrender. The Germans came.

While these two 88's were being knocked out, the rest of 2nd Battalion kept on moving downtown, toward the bridges. Late that morning, the 506th made contact with the British XXX Corps. It was learned that the Guards were still five miles south of Eindhoven, having difficulty with German 88 batteries zeroed in on the highway. Gen. Taylor, who had just then driven up to the Regimental CP, advised that the British be informed of the blown bridge at Son, and asked to put suitable Bailey bridge equipment at the head of the Guards column. This was done.

Then the general asked how things were going in Eindhoven. Col. Sink didn't yet know, having lost radio contact with Col. Strayer and his 2nd Battalion for a time. So, with some trepidation, Col. Sink told Col. Chase, his exec, perched in the Woensel church steeple, to try to get in touch with Strayer. Chase got through, and asked the big question.

Back came Strayer's reply: "We hold the center of town and we are sitting on the four bridges over the Dommel River."

Col. Sink was incredulous at such good news. Gen. Taylor, disbelief on his face also, raced to the top of the steeple to talk to Col. Strayer on the radio himself. Gen. Taylor came down again convinced.

The road was open for the Guards. Eindhoven was free, the first big Dutch city to be liberated. When they realized that the last German was gone, the Dutch went wild, crowding the streets, opening their shops, giving everything they had to the grinning troopers. Amidst the celebrations, the war went on. Defense positions were set up. Patrols went out.

At 12:30 two British armored reconnaissance cars entered the city from the north, having bypassed it during their morning patrol. This was the 101st's first contact with the British. The cars left soon afterward. It is quite probable that these were the very two armored cars that became involved with Wierzbowski and his men later that day.

Not until 6:30 that evening did the troopers of the 506th hear the sound they had been waiting for—the clank of tanks. The Guards Armored Division, looking a bit worse for wear after thirty-six hours of fighting, moved through Eindhoven, and reached Son about nine o'clock. There, members of the 326th Airborne Engineers had been working all day to clear debris from the bridge site. British engineers took over, and during the night they installed the portable Bailey bridges they had brought along for this purpose.

At 6:45 the following morning (thirty-six hours behind schedule) the Guards rumbled across the Bailey bridge and Operation Market-Garden got rolling again, through Son, and on to St. Oedenrode. From St. Oedenrode the Guards thundered on down the highway to Veghel, then beyond Veghel to Grave and the territory of the 82nd Airborne.

The first part of the Screaming Eagles' mission had been accomplished. They had blasted open the road. Now came the second part—keeping the road open. To do this, they had to beat the Germans at Best.

Thus far the 502nd at Best had taken a bad battering, fighting against overwhelming odds. Of course, though they didn't realize it at the time, the troopers had made a valuable contribution to the mission, by sucking enemy reinforcements to Best from all over the Division area. This gave the 501st and 506th a relatively easy time of it.

Now it was time to concentrate on Best. On D plus 1 a glider flight had brought in badly needed reinforcements— two battalions from the 327th Glider Regiment and an assortment of other personnel. Gen. Taylor felt this gave him the means for a major effort—enough of feeding battalions into the action piecemeal and having them chewed up. He set up a task force under Brig. Gen. Gerald J. Higgins (promoted from Colonel) and issued his orders: Best was to be taken with all possible speed and the German garrison there destroyed.

Early on the morning of D plus 2 Col. Chappuis resumed the attack with 2nd Battalion. Immediately the men drew artillery and machine gun fire from the canal area. The advance continued several hundred yards, taking small losses. Then a patrol from Company E reported in with the news that the bridge was blown. In that case, Col. Chappuis saw no point in continuing the attack. He called Regiment. Col. Michaelis told him to dig in where he was and hold. Twice that morning German infantry attacked the battalion. Each time they were driven off with heavy losses.

While 2nd Battalion was thus occupied, Gen. McAuliffe went over to the CP of the 327th Gliders to order the two fresh battalions attached to the 502nd for the battle at Best. At once Lt. Col. Ray C. Allen moved out 3rd Battalion; then he turned the command over to his executive officer while he rushed off by himself to find the 502nd CP.

Looking for it, he stumbled across a group of some 200 German infantry marching south to reinforce the garrison at Best. They opened fire on him. Allen ran for it. He got lucky. The one bullet that "had his name on it" hit a K-ration box in his pocket and stayed there. Allen hastened back to his battalion, intending to deploy it quickly enough to catch and destroy the Germans. But the enemy smelled trouble, broke formation, and hurried on toward Best. Three times groups from 3rd Battalion hit them, each time just a little too late to get them all. But they killed some, and captured 75 stragglers.

About eleven o'clock Allen reported in to the 502nd CP. By that time 2nd Battalion had also arrived, along with a squadron of British tanks assigned to the attack. Gen. Higgins gave each group its assignment. His purpose was to clear all Germans out of the area northeast of the canal and the road. To accomplish this the 502nd, assisted by tanks, would place its right flank on the highway and drive south to the canal. This would take care of the main body of the Germans. To get the numerous groups known to be scattered throughout the nearby forest, 2nd Battalion of the 327th was to push two small forces west and south from Oud Meer, the lake in the middle of the forest. Together they would crush the enemy against the canal. At the same time, 3rd Battalion of the 327th would go north in a move designed to isolate the enemy by the canal.

Major Roy L. Inman, 2nd Battalion CO (327th Gliders) ordered Company G, under Capt. Hugh Evans, to take over the leading role in the attack. The company split, with 1st Platoon going to the right, the rest of the company going left.

The left moved out at 2 P.M., 2nd Platoon out in front. As it followed the road down into the forest, the platoon split into squad groups. Lt. Frank H. Hibbard took the 1st and 2nd Squads along the right side of the road, Tech.-Sgt. Manual Hidalgo took 3rd Squad along the left. The squads advanced along the ditches at the sides of the road until suddenly rifles and machine guns opened up on them. They hit the dirt. Lt. Hibbard sent for two machine guns to be brought forward, then a Browning Automatic Rifle ("BAR").

They didn't help. So Hibbard tried a new double development. He took his men away from the road, 3rd Squad moving off to the right, the other two squads to the left and through the woods. Hibbard and the two squads crawled through the thick undergrowth until they could see and hear a group of seven Germans and a machine gun. One of the glidermen who could understand German said he thought the Germans wanted to surrender. Just then one of the enemy stood up. Someone shot him in the leg. Hibbard yelled, "Cease firing!" But if the Germans had been in a mind to surrender, they were now uncertain of their reception. They wouldn't come out of their positions.

Hibbard's strategy did not call for a frontal assault on a machine gun position. Instead, he moved his two squads around the Germans.

On the other flank, meantime, Sgt. Hidalgo saw a German, with one leg over his bicycle, talking to another man, just off the road. Apparently the noise of the 1st and 2nd Squads moving through the brush had led the Germans to believe no Americans would be coming down the road. Noticing that the German on the bike had his rifle slung over his shoulder, Hidalgo fired over his head. The German jumped a foot in surprise, then recovered, and began pedalling like mad toward the canal. Hidalgo aimed calmly and shot the cyclist in the head with his M1. Then the other German ran to the bicycle and tried to escape with it. Hidalgo shot him in the leg.

By this time all three squads had completed their encirclement of the Germans. Their morale low at this point, the Germans began to rise from their foxholes and surrender—individually and in small groups. Nevertheless, there were still plenty of Germans hiding in the ditches along the road. Then Sgts. Hidalgo and Carl J. Hanlon did a brave thing. The pair of them, in plain sight, walked slowly up and down the middle of the road, calling on the Germans to come out and surrender.

German resistance crumbled. All the Germans rose from their positions with their hands up. Hidalgo, in fact, scored an extra coup with one group he persuaded to give up—he freed an American prisoner, an important one, Major Harry W. Elkins, commanding officer of the 377th Parachute Field Artillery Battalion.

After the prisoners were sent to the rear, the men moved to the canal. There they came upon a small group of buildings in a clearing. The company split into half squads, and began to move through the buildings. They encountered a large group of Germans extremely anxious to surrender. Some of them were so cowed it was thought safe to send a few of their noncommissioned officers into the woods to bring out the rest of the Germans hiding there.

In all, 159 prisoners were taken, and a number of Germans were killed and wounded, without a single casualty being suffered by the company.

Meanwhile, the 502nd was attacking at Best, anxious to avenge the frustrations and defeats of the preceding forty-eight hours. The plan had been for the first British tanks to go to G and I Companies of 3rd Battalion, three tanks to each company. Six tanks would also go to 2nd Battalion. Both battalions were to advance together.

But G Company jumped the gun. It got its tanks first, and, without waiting for anybody else, it started forward toward the German positions, tank cannons blazing. The roar of the cannons and the ominous clanking of the tanks seemed to terrify the enemy. Seventy-five came out of the woods and surrendered. Maj. Stopka, who had run forward to halt the company until I Company was ready, saw what was happening and let G Company get on with it.

A few minutes later I Company got its tanks and moved up behind and alongside G. Six tanks now were sending shells into the woods and at the German positions. Behind them, the troopers flushed the Germans out of the roadside ditches. The Germans had lost heart for this battle. Maj. Stopka realized that this attack was going to work. He radioed Regiment for all the MP's available, to guard the prisoners streaming in. Men up front with the tanks reported that when some of the enemy rose from their fire positions to surrender, they were shot down by their own men.

The advance went all the way to the canal, taking prisoners by the hundreds, sending them back with hardly an escort. During the first two hours of the attack, 2nd Battalion took 700 prisoners. The tanks and the troopers swept through the fields, firing as they went, eliminating any of the enemy who refused to surrender. By evening, some 600 Germans lay dead in the fields around the canal. Eleven hundred surrendered.

That night, the 502nd took up defensive positions from the blown bridge back into the forest. The troopers had broken the back of the Germans at Best. They had avenged their comrades. The position of the Division was now much more secure. As for Best itself, on the other side of the blown bridge, the Screaming Eagles let it be. The enemy was beaten, the flank secured. Capturing Best would be spending troopers' lives needlessly. The mission of the 101st was to open the door for the British armor, clear a sixteen-mile corridor, and keep it clear. The job was done, and would continue to be done.

Unhappily for Operation Market-Garden, the action farther up the corridor was not going so well.

When the Guards Armored Division rumbled north from Veghel on the morning of D plus 2, they expected to find the way clear to Arnhem. The British found that the

82nd Airborne had secured most of its objectives. But it had not been able to capture the crucial bridge across the Waal River at Nijmegen. SS troops, well dug in, were giving the 82nd a hard time of it. Only heroic effort finally took the bridge on D plus 3.

Crossing the Waal the next day, well behind schedule, the Guards Armored found that the Germans had used the extra time to set up defenses along the rest of the road. Further advance was slow and costly.

But that wasn't the half of it. The British at Arnhem, at the top of the corridor, had run into misfortune from the beginning. They landed in an area thick with Germans. Their air drops of supplies fell into enemy hands. Their men, north of the Neder Rijn, failed to seize the bridge that would connect them with the south bank of the river. Without control of that bridge, the Guards Armored would never reach them. By D plus 3 their position was becoming desperate.

Chapter Seven

The Airborne landings in Holland did not come as a complete surprise to the German High Command. Hitler and his generals knew the Allies had large airborne forces ready to be sent into action. Where, they did not know. In weighing the overall situation, they discussed Holland, but concluded that such an adventure was too risky for the Allies to attempt.

Still, when the first paratroopers began to descend, the German High Command saw the significance of what was happening, and began at once to prepare countermeasures. Since the Airborne troops had landed in the sector of the 1st German Parachute Army, its commander, Col. Gen. Kurt Student, was responsible for the immediate response. He made all Luftwaffe units in the area subordinate to the local commanders. Antiaircraft units were formed into battle groups. New fortress battalions were attached to the 1st Parachute Army. By D plus 1 an armored brigade, an assault gun battalion, and two divisions of *Volksgrenadiers* were headed for the corridor.

The German strategy for meeting Market-Garden was to contain the corridor at its base, then cut it just as quickly as possible, in the vicinity of Eindhoven. If this was done after the armored elements had moved north, the British

XXX Corps would be caught in a net and could be systematically destroyed. In any case, Hitler felt the line could be held at Nijmegen, and the corridor cut at some later date.

Not all the German generals agreed with this. Some thought that all the bridges along the way should be destroyed, and the German armies brought back behind the Rhine for a stand. But Field Marshall Walter Model would not hear of it. He had no doubts about the German ability to hold the key bridge at Arnhem. He had enough strength in the area and enough more on the way to stop a crossing of the Rhine in force. While the German armies held there, at the very top of the corridor, counterattacks would be made all along the corridor in an attempt to cut the lifeline.

For the Screaming Eagles, the second phase of their Holland Operation was about to begin: defending the corridor. Division leaders knew from the beginning how easy it might be for the Germans to cut the corridor, and what a disastrous effect such a stroke would have on the entire operation. It was obviously good German strategy to stop the flow of traffic somewhere near the base of the corridor and then deal at leisure with the American and British forces up north at Nijmegen and Arnhem.

Division knew this, but it also knew that there was no real defense against any strong German group that was determined to grab a stretch of road. The Division was spread too thinly. Parts of the road were completely unguarded. It was a dilemma. The road couldn't be defended by sitting still and letting the enemy organize his strength for an overwhelming attack at a single point. At the same time, aggressive patrolling and battalion-sized attacks were also a calculated risk. If too many men spent too much time roaming around the countryside looking for a fight, the Division as a whole might suffer, become disorganized, and be weakened. Gen. Taylor saw this happen at Best, when a platoon-sized action developed into a regimental commitment. Had the Germans mounted a strong attack on the highway while most of the 502nd was tied up at Best, they could have cut the corridor with ease.

There was no one answer to this dilemma. Much depended on the situation as it developed and as it was seen by the unit commanders. In addition, the Eagles were beginning to get helpful information from the Dutch Underground about German troop movements. Thus there were times when Gen. Taylor or one of his regimental commanders might feel it safe to take aggressive action with large units, confident that the Germans had not set them up for a trap.

In any case, from D plus 3 it was evident that strong German groups were in the Division area. The only question was where and when they would strike to cut the corridor. To keep the 101st off balance, the Germans kept up the pressure at several spots at once, waiting for the right moment to launch their main attack.

On the morning of D plus 3 (September 20) the German *107th Panzers* pounced on Son. They moved in strength against Company C of the 327th, which was holding a 400-yard front south of the Wilhelmina Canal with only its headquarters group, its 1st Platoon, and its light machine gun and mortar sections. The outpost that first gave the alarm was wiped out, and Company Commander Capt. William L. Miller had to shift his men rapidly from place to place to stop an immediate breakthrough. Fortunately, the terrain was flat, and the two German tanks leading the assault were afraid to get too close. Company C held. Then the Germans shifted their attack north of the canal, held by 1st Battalion of the 506th. This attack also was beaten off.

An hour later the Germans renewed their assault on the 327th, this time with more infantry and eight tanks. A bitter fight ensued. The lines began to give. More men were needed desperately. Thirty clerks and headquarters men from the 506th came marching by—they were pressed into the fight. Suddenly ten British tanks appeared from the direction of Best. The two lead tanks were knocked out when they ran over an American mine field, despite attempts by Company C men to warn them. The remaining eight took on the German tanks and destroyed four of them, losing one of their own.

By midmorning a general German retreat had started. For a time the enemy had interrupted traffic on the road, but they had never quite cut it.

A few miles north, at St. Oedenrode, the Germans also kept the 101st busy. Batteries of 88's and self-propelled guns shelled the town sporadically, making movement hazardous. Under this intermittent fire, 2nd and 3rd Battalions of the 502nd moved away from their positions at Best and into St. Oedenrode. At the same time, an advance detail was preparing an old castle in the town for use as the Division Command Post, Gen. Taylor deciding that Son was no longer safe. During the shelling, one burst made a direct hit on the 1st Battalion CP, killing four men and wounding two others. At that point Col. Cassidy moved out and into the basement of an old factory. Then he took two British tanks and a squad of men and drove off the enemy guns.

For the first time since the drop, the 502nd was united. It took over responsibility for the St. Oedenrode area. For the first time, too, the troopers had artillery behind them. Gliders brought in several batteries of howitzers and the artillerymen to man them.

Still farther north along the road, around Veghel, the initiative was taken by the 501st, not the Germans. Col. Johnson, in accord with the general strategy of aggressive patrolling, decided it would be more effective to outpost his area strongly rather than keep all his forces concentrated passively in one place. So he sent 3rd Battalion south to Eerde and Company C of 1st Battalion north to Heeswijk-Dinther.

Another move was made which later events were to make especially fortunate. The Medical Company sent an attached platoon of the 50th Field Hospital forward to Veghel to establish an aid station there. Later a surgical team was sent up to join them. They were shortly to get more work than they could handle.

Once his outposts were in place, Col. Johnson gave Col. Kinnard permission to use all of 1st Battalion for a killing sweep up to the town of Heeswijk. The object was to destroy any enemy forces his patrols could find. To accomplish this, Kinnard set into motion a broom-and-dustpan operation. Company C was ordered to be the dustpan, taking positions extending from a point to the south of Heeswijk up to the drawbridge over the Willems Vaart Canal. Companies A and B would act as the broom, sweeping up to C, driving the Germans ahead of them into C's killing zone.

Company B went forward as the left side of the broom, with the canal as its left hand boundary. Several hundred yards to the right was Company A. Capt. Stanfield A. Stach of Company A had his men move out on either side of the Aa River, 2nd Platoon on the left bank, 3rd Platoon on the right, with 1st in reserve, also on the right. A light machine gun section from HQ Company marched behind 2nd Platoon.

Stach wasn't too crazy about having his platoon split by the river, or for that matter, having the wide gap between the two assault companies. To reduce this problem, he ordered his extreme left hand squad to maintain a continuing patrol between A and B. But this squad soon became lost, and was rendered useless in the action that followed.

The advance moved ahead without opposition for perhaps

half an hour. Then, from a windmill on the right bank, a machine gun opened up on the troopers on the opposite side of the river. The men dropped quickly and no one was hit. Stach went forward along with Lt. Billy Turner of 2nd Platoon, which was under fire, and Lt. George Murn. While they were working their way across a field they noticed four Germans in the weeds about a hundred yards ahead. Stach called out for them to surrender. Instead they jumped into a drainage ditch and disappeared.

Figuring he must be close to the German line, Stach called back for two of his machine guns and set them in position forward. Then he and the two lieutenants crawled ahead through a pasture till they saw a line of trees with flanking ditches providing good cover. They thought this was the enemy position. And they were right. When they advanced a bit further heavy rifle and machine gun fire broke out.

Stach crawled back under fire and deployed his men. He sent one rifle squad and one machine gun into the position he'd just vacated. The other machine gun he put on his left flank to cover the area separating his unit from Company B. Under pressure from the machine guns, the German fire fell off. But Stach knew he couldn't do much more without help from the other platoons. He sent a runner to 1st Platoon with word that it was to cross the river near the windmill, where he'd spotted a wooden bridge. Then, anxious to get going with the attack, he crossed the Aa himself, detached a squad from 3rd Platoon, and brought it back with him.

Stach sent this squad, together with 1st Platoon, up along the right flank of the enemy positions. At the same time, he signalled to Lt. Turner to let the Germans have it with every gun he had. Under the cover of fire from Turner's group, Stach and the rest moved from ditch to ditch, closer to the German front line. And then, throwing caution to the winds, Lt. Cecil O. Fuquay and six men rose from cover and charged out into the open, yelling and firing as they ran. This courageous charge stampeded the Germans. They rose from their ditches and ran.

At this Lt. Turner stood up, exposed himself to enemy fire, and yelled to the Germans to come back and surrender. Some of the Germans stopped running and did just that. Encouraged, Turner ran on to the next field and repeated his demand. This time he was answered with a bullet in the head. He died instantly. Pfc. John C. Webb, up there right along with Turner, was also cut down and killed.

While 2nd Platoon and the rest were thus engaged on the left bank of the river, the remaining two squads of 3rd Platoon advanced and silenced the machine in the windmill. When word of this got to Capt. Stach, he ordered 3rd Platoon Leader Lt. Henry J. Pulhaski to press on to the outskirts of the village of Dinther. As the men moved forward they came under fire from both sides of the river. But then two Germans directly to the front of 3rd Platoon got up and waved white handkerchiefs. Pulhaski walked forward. From somewhere a shot rang out. It triggered a volley of fire from the German lines. Pulhaski fell dead, riddled with bullets.

The advance of Company A came to a halt as German resistance stiffened around a big red barn and communicating ditches. But help soon arrived from Company B, despite the absence of communication between them. This company had advanced steadily along the canal. It had destroyed three 20mm guns, suffered only light casualties, and then found itself along a line of ditches, off to the left of the same red barn Company A was trying to reach.

Now the Germans came under a two-pronged attack. This new assault persuaded them to quit. Fifty Germans came out of the red barn, hands in the air. When they surrendered, all the other Germans in the ditches got up and surrendered. The back of German resistance had been broken. Two reinforced companies had been in and around the red barn. All were now dead or wounded, were prisoners, or were fleeing in panic toward the rear—where the dustpan, Company C, lay in waiting.

Capt. Robert H. Phillips had to rout a few Germans before he could get his dustpan into position. He killed a few and captured many more, including a battalion commander. When he was set, he spread his company out in a line from the canal, through the Aa River banks, over the river's drawbridge, and up to a roadblock he set up in front of the village of Heeswijk (about a mile west of Dinther). During the morning hours he didn't get much business, just a few stragglers retreating before the attack by A and B Companies. But about three in the afternoon he got what he was waiting for—hordes of Germans came a-running, all those who hadn't been killed or made prisoner in the battle around the red barn.

With a rush these Germans made for a wooded area near the canal. But Capt. Phillips had thoughtfully placed a machine gun to cover that exit. The gun caught the enemy on the flank and mowed them down. The Germans hesitated, stopped. A few then began to shout "Kamerad." But they held onto their weapons. Capt. Phillips sent a messenger out to them saying that they'd have to put their weapons down or he'd fire. The messenger returned. "They said they have plenty of time," he related to Capt. Phillips. "They say it's too early in the day to surrender."

During these negotiations the American guns were quiet. Angrily, Phillips yelled out, "I'm going to kill every damned one of you." With that he signalled for everything to let go at once. Machine guns, rifles, Tommy guns, and mortars cut into the German ranks. Within five minutes the enemy was clinging to the earth, throwing their rifles and burp guns in the air in surrender. Capt. Phillips ordered his men to cease firing.

Those Germans who were left alive rose and came into the American positions. There were more than a hundred of them, dragging 40 wounded along. Others kept coming in, as A and B Companies moved steadily forward, sweeping all before them. By 5:30 that evening it was all over. Losing only four men killed and six wounded, the battalion had killed forty Germans, wounded many more, and taken 418 prisoners.

On the fifth day of Operation Market-Garden (D plus 4) German pressure on the 101st eased a bit. As many suspected, this was just the calm before the storm. But the troopers used this respite to good advantage. For the first three days of the campaign there had been no evacuation of casualties. This was due to the heavy volume of northbound traffic. But on the fourth day ambulances and trucks came through the lines; on the fifth day, as the fighting slowed, these vehicles loaded with the wounded went back to an evacuation hospital in Belgium.

Gen. Taylor took steps to move some of his men north, as the British moved more men into the base of the corridor and took over some of the defensive positions there. Taylor also wanted to widen the corridor as much as he could, keeping the Germans outside artillery range of the road, and making it more difficult for them to effect a complete cut.

Taylor left only E and F Companies of 2nd Battalion (506th) in the Eindhoven area, the southernmost base of the 101st. He sent D Company of the 2nd plus A Company of the 1st Battalion four miles to the northeast, to the town of Nuenen. The two companies took and held the town without a fight.

Companies B and C of 1st Battalion moved north five miles

into Son, then got orders from Division to move out of Son and march quickly to Uden, which lay astride the road about three miles northeast of Veghel. Up to that point, the Division hadn't attempted to defend the road north of Veghel up to the limits of the 82nd's section, although Uden was technically in its zone. Neither had the Germans made any moves in that area.

Col. Sink, the 506th's CO, made a reconnaissance and decided to move 175 men and some machine guns and mortars to Uden early the next morning. He shifted 3rd Battalion to St. Oedenrode, where it went into Division reserve. With that battalion in town, Col. Michaelis at St. Oedenrode got his 502nd Regiment together and pushed them out in a horseshoe shaped movement, open end to the east. He had under his command a squadron of British tanks, which he distributed among his three battalions.

Col. Cassidy's 1st Battalion moved out from St. Oedenrode along the road leading northwest toward the town of Schijndel. During the course of some heavy fighting along the road, he received word from the Dutch Underground that the Germans were planning a major attack from the direction of Schijndel. The report indicated that a large German convoy with some two thousand men had already left Schijndel and was moving in the direction of St. Oedenrode.

To block the German attack Gen. Taylor made plans to strike the enemy in the rear. Two battalions of the 501st (1st and 3rd) were ordered to attack Schijndel while the men of the 502nd continued their advance up the road. The two units would meet and crush the Germans between them. Making an extremely difficult night advance, Col. Kinnard and Col. Ewell got to Schijndel and secured the town against light opposition.

So as D plus 5 dawned, the Screaming Eagles thought they were in excellent position for an annihilating attack upon the large German group south of Schijndel. Two battalions of the 501st were behind them, ready to move south; two battalions of the 502nd were in front of the Germans, ready to move north.

Only it didn't happen that way.

The blow the 101st had been expecting for two days fell that morning. A German attack cut the road between Veghel and Uden. When the word was radioed to Kinnard and Ewell, with it came an order to send back all the British tanks; they were needed elsewhere. The encirclement of the Germans south of Schijndel could not continue as planned. All four battalions eventually abandoned the attack and headed back toward the corridor between Veghel and St. Oedenrode.

So a day that began with high hopes of a brilliant offensive became instead a day of desperate defense.

Chapter Eight

It's likely the Germans chose Veghel as the point of their attack because the destruction of the bridges over the Aa River and the Zuid-Willems Vaart Canal would halt all traffic along the corridor long after the attackers might have gone. They probably had no idea that because of the maneuvers around Schinjdel, Veghel was being held only by 2nd Battalion of the 501st.

The Dutch Underground managed to get word to Division that morning about large German forces moving toward the corridor at Veghel, but by then nothing much could be done about it. The Germans had a 400-truck convoy moving in from the east, composed of units from the *107th Panzers* and the *280th Assault Gun Brigade*. From the west a large infantry force with five mobile guns was approaching along both banks of the canal, ready to strike. At about 9:30 in the morning, the enemy launched a coordinated attack on Veghel from the southeast, the north, and the northwest. It started the biggest battle thus far in Holland.

When the assault began, the advance party from 1st Battalion, the 506th, was already on its way to Uden, north of Veghel. Riding trucks, jeeps, and any other kind of vehicle they could muster, the troopers rushed north, commanded by Col. Charles Chase, the regimental executive officer. They arrived in Uden at 11 o'clock, just in time to be cut off and isolated by the Germans, who cut the road below them. Fortunately, the Germans didn't know that Col. Chase had only little more than a company of men with him, or they could easily have overwhelmed him. The colonel shrewdly shifted his men back and forth around the town, creating the impression of a larger force. His bluff worked; the Germans never tried an all-out attack against him.

In Veghel itself, Gen. McAuliffe was in charge of the defense. He had come up to the town that morning to find a new site for the Division CP. When the attack broke, Gen. Taylor told him to stay on and take over. Shortly after eleven, the men of 2nd Battalion, 501st, saw the tanks and infantry of the *107th Panzers* advancing along the road that led east to the town of Erp. The battle was on.

Greatly outnumbered and outgunned, the troopers met the assault from foxholes and houses at the outskirts of town. The first wave of the enemy broke over them. With bazookas and mortars they checked the tanks. When the infantry came in close with their rifles, grenades, and burp guns, troopers held fast, poured all the fire they could muster on the enemy, and drove back that first wave.

That was the best they could do for the moment. Helplessly, they saw part of the German column swing around their left toward the road to Uden and cut it. There was nobody there to stop them. Then the Germans wheeled and attacked Veghel down the Uden road as well. The situation was becoming desperate when 2nd Battalion of the 506th rode into town from the south. Gen. McAuliffe rushed them to the northern perimeter in time to battle the Germans coming from the Uden road. With 2nd Battalion was a group from the 81st Airborne Antiaircraft Battalion, towing their 57mm guns—useful as antitank weapons.

Spotting Col. Cox, the 81st's CO, Gen. McAuliffe shouted

to him, "Get one of your guns up that road and smash a tank. That may stop them!"

Col. Cox jumped into the nearest of his gun-towing jeeps and told the driver to get going. In the jeep were Capt. Adolph Gueymard, Cpl. William Bowyer, and PFC. Rogie Roberts. Together they raced up the Uden road toward the sound of firing. A sad sight greeted them. A German Mark V Panther tank was astride the road, shooting up a British Antiaircraft unit which had been caught on the road when the attack began. This unit was equipped only with 37mm guns. Strangely, as Col. Cox arrived on the scene, there was a 37mm, manned by an American crew from the 327th, duelling with the German tank. Nobody knew how they got there, mixed with the British, but there they were. And their duel was a valiant, but hopeless one. Shooting 37mm shells at a German Panther was about as useful as throwing rocks at it.

Col. Cox wasted no time looking for protection. He and his crew swung their 57 around in the middle of the road, about 100 yards from the tank. The Germans saw them and fired. The gun crew saw the flash from the cannon, but luckily the shell sailed over their heads and hit a house behind them, starting a shower of masonry. Calmly Col. Cox squinted through the gun sights, aimed, and fired. The shot knocked some treads off the tank, crippling it. His second quick shot set the tank on fire.

That setback for the moment took some of the steam out of the German attack. But they were by no means stopped. They slid around 2nd Battalion to the left, continuing the pressure in a northern arc around Veghel. More help was needed—and fast.

And it was coming. The 327th was on its way. But because the corridor in their area was still clogged with heavy British traffic northbound, the glidermen were forced onto secondary roads. This delayed their march. When Col. Harper and his 327th reached St. Oedenrode, they learned that the attack on Veghel was well under way and the situation serious. Gathering what motor transport he could, Col. Harper loaded his mortars, antitank guns, heavy machine guns, two companies from 3rd Battalion and another battery from the 81st Antiaircraft Battalion, and roared north up the main road to Veghel. They got there about one in the afternoon, and at once moved into defense positions on the left flank of 2nd Battalion, 506th. Together, the two groups successfully beat off the Germans and cleared a space in the road.

An hour later the Germans hit from the west, moving against the highway bridge over the canal. With their heavy mobile artillery they cleared the bridge area. Gen. McAuliffe and Col. Sink hurried over to see what could be done. On the way they ran into Company D of the 506th (2nd Battalion) headed for Uden, unaware that the road was cut. They turned the company around and brought it with them to the bridge area. Just as this unit arrived a group of Sherman tanks clanked up from the south, headed right for the bridge. The tankers did not know that the German guns had it completely covered. If they got onto the bridge they'd be sitting ducks.

There was only one way to stop them—and Col. Sink did it. He ran across the bridge through a hail of small arms fire and stopped the tanks in time.

The presence of the tanks, the fresh troopers, and the stubborn defense of the bridge discouraged the Germans. They broke off the attack, then swung around to the south to cut the road between Veghel and St. Oedenrode, which would complete the encirclement of Veghel. But just as they were effecting the cut on the highway, the balance of the 327th Gliders and the 321st Artillery came marching up the road from St. Oedenrode. Quickly A and C Companies deployed and advanced against the German right flank, firing as they came on.

The Germans broke and headed west, back along the canal. The two assault companies kept pushing until the road was clear and they had joined the men fighting at the vital bridge. Seventy prisoners were rounded up. The road south was open again. The bridge was for the moment safe from enemy attack.

All day long and on into the night the Germans attacked, were beaten back, came on again, and were again repulsed. The town of Veghel was plastered steadily with artillery. The Dutch civilians, so overjoyed by their deliverance several days before, were now huddled in their cellars, praying that something of their little town would be left standing when the battle was over.

Meanwhile, troopers were stranded in Uden. Where the Germans had cut the road north of Veghel, they had brought disaster to everything they'd caught on it. Burning British vehicles of every description littered the road. Trucks by the dozen, loaded with vital supplies for the troops at Nijmegen and Arnhem, were looted or destroyed.

Cutting the road was like cutting an artery leading to the heart of Operation Market-Garden. The road north would have to be opened. The Germans would have to be denied the two vital bridges over the Aa and over the canal.

The next morning the Germans again attacked from the south and from the west, trying for the canal bridge. Again they were stopped. Then the Eagles counterattacked. Two battalions of the 506th moved out astride the road north to Uden. Before their determined onslaught the Germans faded. The troopers advanced more than a mile up the road; there they encountered forward elements of the British Grenadier Guards, moving down from the north. The road was open. The men in Uden were safe. With the corridor clear, the troopers turned their attention to the Germans west and southeast of Veghel. They attacked the enemy concentrations at both points and drove them back.

However, the battle was not done. For four more days it seesawed back and forth. Down from the northwest came a strong German force, aiming at cutting the road again between Veghel and St. Oedenrode, near the town of Koevring. The enemy threw in the best it had. Into battle marched men of the *6th* and *1st Parachute Regiments* and units from the crack *Hermann Goering Division*. On the sand dunes near the town of Eerde the pride of the German *Wermacht* met the troopers of the 501st, and they were defeated.

But a small group, some 200 men and a few tanks, slipped away from the field of battle, found an unprotected road, and hit Koevring. They caught a British convoy, knocked out three tanks, burnt all the trucks, and cut the road at that point. Again the corridor was blocked. For the next 24 hours this small but strong German force held the highway against counterattack. It came down to tank against tank, man against man. Units from the 502nd, the 506th, and the British Queen's Guards got the Germans in a vise and began squeezing.

At darkness the next day, what remained of the German force sneaked away to the northwest. Behind them, they left a road so choked with mines that it took the 326th Engineers another half day of dangerous work to clear the road for traffic. Not until the eleventh day of Operation Market-Garden could the troopers of the 101st take a deep breath and believe that, for the moment at least, their part of the battle was over and won. Traffic up and down their part of the corridor ran freely. There was even mail from England. Barbers in Veghel were cuttting hair. A few men got passes to Brussels.

Some men of the 101st actually believed that the Screaming Eagles would be relieved and sent back to England. The campaign had already gone on many more days than scheduled. The Eagles, after all, were a "strike force" unit, not an ordinary infantry division. But their days in Holland were far from over. While they had been fighting around Veghel to keep the lifeline open, what had been happening up north determined their fate for the next two months.

Ever since D plus 3, when the bridge at Nijmegen had been seized, the British XXX Corps had been trying to force a pathway north from the Waal River to the Neder Rijn (Lower Rhine). But rainy weather made the fields impassable to tanks. The road at that point was like the causeway that plagued the 101st at Carentan—it stood out several feet above the flat countryside. Tanks moving along it were like ducks in a shooting gallery to the German 88's. British progress was costly and slow.

Finally, on D plus 5, a group of light armored cars managed to cut loose and make an end run around to Driel, on the south bank of the river, not far from Arnhem. There they joined forces with a group of Polish paratroopers who had been dropped there. On the north bank of the river, at Arnhem, was the British 1st Airborne Division, completely surrounded by an overwhelming force of Germans. Day by day the circle closed and gallant men died in fierce, bloody fighting, until the remnants of the division were confined in a small area just west of Arnhem and north of the river.

The continued resistance of the British in a hopeless situation lives on in history as one of the most heroic and tragic episodes of the war.

On D plus 8, under cover of night, the survivors were pulled back across the river, under the constant threat of complete annihilation. Of the 10,095 men who marched or dropped into the battle, 2,490 came back across the river. The British had indeed tried to venture, "a bridge too far."

The Allied High Command gave up on the idea of reaching the Zuyder Zee. It was accepted that the south bank of the Lower Rhine would be the northern limit of Operation Market-Garden.

In effect, the Operation as planned was a failure. It did not accomplish what it had set out to do. Allied troops were not across the Rhine. The Siegfried Line was not outflanked. Still, on the positive side, it could be honestly said that the Operation had liberated large areas of Holland and had advanced the northern flank of Allied forces sixty-five miles.

Certainly the troopers of the 101st had done their part. They had seized and then held open their part of the corridor for a much longer period than originally planned, but not without cost. During the first 11 days of the campaign the division had 373 men killed, 1,436 wounded, and 547 missing in action.

But the 101st could not be recalled for a rest. The British, weakened as they were by the disaster at Arnhem, needed help to maintain the new front line along the Lower Rhine. When the situation along the southern part of the corridor had become stabilized, the 101st was sent north to take over a line of defense extending east to west for ten miles, from the town of Opheusden on the west to Elst on the east.

There, on that section of flat, wet ground that came to be called "The Island," the Division spent two miserable months. From the north bank of the river, where the terrain was hilly, the German artillery could look right down the throats of the troopers. Daytime movement of any kind was dangerous. Supply vehicles ran a gauntlet of shell fire to reach the front. It was almost like the terrible trench warfare of World War I—foxholes that filled with water, bad food, constant sniping, shelling, dying. A war of attrition. Of artillery duels. Here the troopers for the first time met the new "Screaming Meemies," the German multibarreled mortars that screeched shrilly as they sent their shells skyward.

Early in October, during the course of a German attack, Col. Johnson was killed by an artillery shell. That left only Col. Sink of the original regimental commanders. Col. Ewell was made the new CO of the 501st. He named Lt. Col. George M. Griswold CO of his old battalion, the 3rd. Col. Ballard he made his exec, giving Ballard's 2nd Battalion to Maj. Sammie Homan.

Gen. Taylor, too, narrowly missed death on "The Island." On November 9 he was wounded by a mortar round.

For the men of the 101st, the dull, dangerous days seemed to go on and on. They pulled patrol, they cursed the German artillery, the cold, the dampness. They couldn't believe they would stay there through the winter, their morale slowly ebbing, their numbers slowly dwindling, eroding under the merciless abrasion of the German artillery and relentless sniping.

At last, in mid-November, their relief began. Unit by unit the Division was pulled out of the line in Holland and sent to Mourmelon-le-Grand, near the city of Reims, France. There, in what was once a French artillery garrison, the Division was to rest, refit, train replacements, and wait for the next call back to action.

Even as the advance parties were rolling into Mourmelon-le-Grand, destiny was again rolling the dice for the 101st Airborne. Once again their numbers would come up. For, in an underground bunker in East Prussia, deep within a dark forest, Hitler and his generals were putting the finishing touches to a plan that would force the troopers from their comfortable garrison all too soon.

A tremendous offensive was being prepared. Code name: *Wacht am Rhein,* Watch on the Rhine. The result of this, Hitler's last mad gamble to win the war, would be the momentous, history-making Battle of the Bulge. The Screaming Eagles would help to write that history, indeed play the vital part in it, with an exhibition of superb, unflinching courage in a Belgian city they would make forever famous: Bastogne.

PART III

THE BATTLE
OF THE BULGE

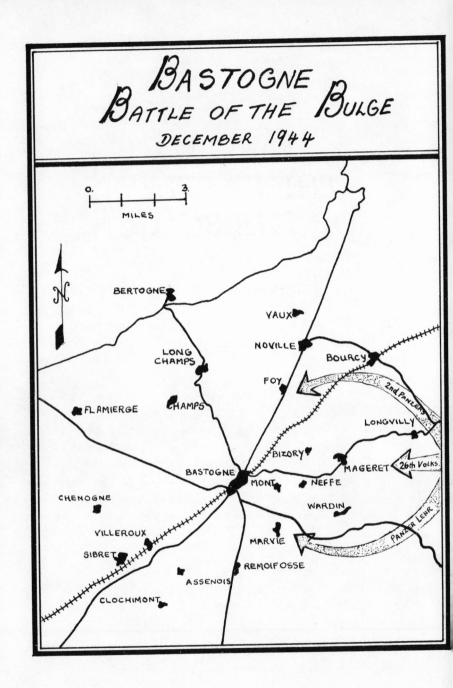

BASTOGNE
BATTLE OF THE BULGE
DECEMBER 1944

0. ————————— 3.
MILES

N

BERTOGNE

VAUX

NOVILLE

LONG CHAMPS

BOURCY

FOY

2nd PANZER

FLAMIERGE

CHAMPS

LONGVILLY

BIZORY

MAGERET

26th VOLKS

BASTOGNE

MONT

NEFFE

CHENOGNE

WARDIN

PANZER LEHR

VILLEROUX

MARVIE

SIBRET

REMOIFOSSE

ASSENOIS

CLOCHIMONT

Chapter Nine

By early summer of 1944 a number of the German General Staff accepted the fact that the war was lost. Once the combined American-British-Canadian armies had landed in France and successfully enlarged their beachhead areas, these senior officers realized there would be no stopping them. Further, the German armies in Italy had been pushed back to their last line of defense, the Gothic Line, north of Florence; on the Eastern Front the Russians were advancing steadily against collapsing German strength.

To these elite of the *Wermacht,* there seemed no point in going on with the war, with the killing, and with the destruction of more millions of German soldiers and civilians. The areas of German conquest were shrinking rapidly, and soon the soil of Germany itself would become the battlefield. The victorious Allied Armies would be marching through the smoldering ruins of German towns and villages, just as the *Wermacht* had marched through the rest of Europe for five triumphant years.

These German officers, proud professional soldiers all, saw a chance to save Germany from total destruction, saw a chance to gain a negotiated peace from the Allies. It would mean getting rid of Hitler; while the Fuhrer was alive the Allies would not budge from their demand for Germany's "unconditional surrender."

They devised a plot to kill Hitler. On July 20, 1944, Count Felix von Stauffenberg, Chief of Staff of the *Wermacht's* Replacement Army, placed a bomb in a briefcase in the conference room of Hitler's headquarters in East Prussia. Ten minutes after von Stauffenberg left the room, the bomb went off. Miraculously, Hitler escaped with minor injuries. The plotters were uncovered and executed.

Predictably, the attempt on his life strengthened Hitler's resolve to go on with the war, even "to the last drop of German blood." What was more, he would win it. Bedridden for a time, recuperating from his injuries, Hitler daydreamed of a master stroke that would destroy Germany's enemies. He knew that the badly mauled *Wermacht* had to regain the initiative. Some brilliant counteroffensive would have to be conceived.

To give the devil his due, Hitler had his moments of strategic daring, perhaps even genius. He knew his way around a military situation map. He had a tremendous grasp of detail. Until the last months of the war, when he completely lost touch with reality, he could plan a campaign down to the last company marching order.

Now he believed that he alone represented Germany's chance for survival. He could no longer trust his generals. He himself would conceive a plan that would turn the war around and once more put the armies of the Third Reich on the road to victory.

He decided that his best chance lay in inflicting a smashing defeat upon the Allies on the Western Front. Not upon the Russians. The Russians could absorb incredible losses of men like a sponge. But a stunning blow to the Americans, British, and Canadians could well shake their confidence and make them see reason, agree to peace terms, withdraw from the war, and leave Germany free to beat the Russians unhampered.

But where to attack? Hitler studied the maps.

While he studied and pondered through the summer months and into early autumn, the Allied race across France, Holland, and Belgium sputtered to a halt. The Germans began to hold all along the line, partly because they now had their backs to the wall of their own country, partly because the rapid Allied advance had outdistanced the supply lines. Everything was short: gasoline, ammunition, rations, replacements. With the failure of Operation Market-Garden, the entire Western Front became more or less stabilized. Both sides took advantage of the comparative lull in the fighting for a deep breath.

Along the nearly 500 miles of the British-American front, units were shuffled here and there, worn out divisions replaced with fresh ones, replacements fed into the front lines to give them combat experience, and preparations made for new winter offensives on the northern and southern extremes of the long front.

The Germans were not idle during this period. By Hitler's direct order a new Army was created, called the *Sixth Panzer Army,* headed by Hitler's old friend, Gen. Sepp Dietrich. This was the Army that would be held in reserve until the decision was made about the grand offensive. Four crack SS Panzer Divisions were to form the nucleus of this new Army: the *Liebstandarte,* the *Hitler Jugend* (Hitler Youth), the *Das Reich,* and the *Hohenstaufen.* Other divisions would be added. Hitler ordered a massive call-up of reserves, a veritable scraping of the bottom of Germany's manpower barrel. The *Luftwaffe* and naval training stations were closed down, the men diverted to Infantry divisions. Boys of sixteen and men in their forties and fifties were pressed into uniform, many with physical impairments that formerly kept them out of the services.

One way or the other, Hitler intended to have his Legions.

And then Hitler saw where he would attack: the Ardennes. Here, in the heavily wooded hills where the borders of Belgium, Luxembourg, and Germany meet—here he would hurl his lightning bolt. The new German armies would attack over ground made holy by German history: it was through these same forests that German armies had attacked victoriously in the Franco-Prussian War in 1870, in World War I in 1914, and again in 1940.

Tradition was not the principal reason for Hitler's choice. Intelligence reports told him this was the weakest sector on the entire Allied front. Only three divisions held a sector roughly eighty miles long, when normally a division would not be asked to hold more than a five-mile front. The undermanned Ardennes sector was considered a calculated risk by the American High Command, because it was a "quiet sector." It had natural obstacles which made it a bit easier to defend, the Germans were thought to be weak on the opposite front, and, in any case, troops were badly needed elsewhere for the coming offensives in the Ruhr to the north and in France to the south.

In the center sector of these three divisions was the green, fresh-from-the-states 106th, the Golden Lions. On their left flank was the 99th; on their right flank, the 28th. On the extreme edges of this front, and destined to be brought into the battle looming ahead, were the 2nd Infantry Division on the left of the 99th, and on the extreme right, the 9th Armored and the 4th Infantry Divisions. All told the strength of these divisions was some 83,000 men and 242 tanks.

Secretly lining up against them on the German side of the forest were 700 tanks and 250,000 men. Their order of battle called for the new *Sixth Panzer* to attack on the extreme northern sector (the American left flank). In the center would be the *Fifth Panzer Army*. In the south, the *Seventh German Army*. The overall purpose of this *blitzkrieg* was the destruction of the three Allied armies that lay in front of the offensive, and, eventually, the recapture of the port of Antwerp. This called for an advance of roughly 120 miles for the Germans. Privately, most of Hitler's field commanders thought they would be lucky to go half that distance, to the River Meuse. But even that would be a serious setback to the Allies.

On December 15, all was ready.

Much has been written since the war about the ability of the Germans to build up such massive forces in the Ardennes without being discovered by Allied intelligence. There were, after all, constant reconnaissance flights over the area, infantry patrols, prisoners being taken and interrogated. There were plenty of hints at a big push in the offing. But these bits and pieces of information were discounted when weighed against a preconceived conviction that in the first place, the Germans no longer had the ability, the manpower, or the machinery to launch a major counterattack anywhere; secondly, if they were to try such an attack, it would come in the north, around Aachen.

To give the Germans credit, they did accomplish an incredible feat of logistics in strict secrecy, with an optimum of security. Men and supplies were brought in from as far away as Norway, Italy, and the Russian front. By December 15, seventeen infantry and armored divisions were ready to jump off on the Ardennes offensive. As far as the Allied High Command knew, there were only seven German divisions on that front.

At 5:30 on the morning of December 16, 1944, the Germans struck.

Through the early morning fog and freezing mist, a quarter of a million German soldiers advanced toward the thinly held American lines, preceded by a massive artillery bombardment. They achieved complete surprise and quick success. GI's in their foxholes were rudely awakened by the crash of shells, the clank of tank treads, the chatter of machine guns. Advance outposts were overrun. Communication lines were destroyed. All along the eighty mile front the enemy thrust penetrated the American lines.

As the first shock wave of the enemy attack rolled over them, the GI's and their officers fought back blindly and instinctively. Even the green soldiers of the 106th put up a grim fight. But all was confusion. The surprise and the lack of communication led each unit along the front to believe it was the object of a localized attack. At Supreme Headquarters in Versailles, Eisenhower and his staff gathered in the growing mountain of reports and gradually grasped the true picture: the Germans had launched an all-out offensive. Penetrations of from two to four miles had been made. Battalions had disappeared. Entire regiments were threatened with envelopment and annihilation.

By the morning of the 17th, the situation had worsened substantially. Divisions were shifted from the north and south to the Ardennes. But they would not be enough. A major breakthrough was imminent unless the Germans could be stopped. Already an ominous "bulge" was appearing on the situation map at American HQ. More men were needed. More divisions. All available reserves would have to be hurled into the battle to plug the holes, to contain the "bulge."

That was a problem. Reserves. There were only two divisions available in reserve, the 82nd and the 101st Airborne Divisions. Eisenhower and his generals hesitated. Both divisions were battle weary, barely three weeks out of the shattering campaign in Holland. The 101st's commander, Gen. Taylor, was in Washington for a conference. The assistant division commander and many other senior officers were in England on leave. The division was temporarily under command of the artillery CO, Gen. McAuliffe.

Still, it couldn't be helped. Both paratroop divisions would have to go into battle again. By truck.

At 8:30 on the evening of the 17th, a call was put through to Lt. Col. Ned D. Moore, 101st Chief of Staff. The Screaming Eagles were to mount up and get going for the town of Werbomont, in Belgium.

Half an hour later Gen. McAuliffe got the entire staff together and told them of the order. "All I know of the situation is that there has been a breakthrough," he said. "And we have got to get up there."

Not until the following morning, as the troopers began piling into huge trailer trucks, did word get to England about the 101st's marching orders. In a London hotel, Col. Sink and Col. Harper were quietly having breakfast when a message arrived from Mourmelon-le-Grand. They were to return immediately by fastest transport available.

Col. Sink looked at Col. Harper knowingly. "Well, Bud," he said to Harper, "here we go again."

Chapter Ten

Gen. McAuliffe was not a man to waste time. Leaving his staff to supervise the loading and movement of the division, he grabbed a command car and just before noon on the 18th sped to the front, taking with him his aide, Lt. Frederic D. Starrett, and Col. Kinnard. The general wanted to see for himself what the story was before his troops got to the battlefield.

As the command car neared a road junction some twenty-five miles southest of Werbomont, Gen. McAuliffe made a snap and, as it turned out, fortuitous decision. Instead of continuing north to Werbomont, he decided to head for the town of Bastogne.

At Bastogne was Maj. Gen. Troy Middleton, commander of VIII Corps. McAuliffe thought it would be a good idea to have himself briefed by the area commander on the general situation. When the car reached the road junction, Gen. McAuliffe stopped and verified directions at a Military Police post. Another lucky decision.

It was four o'clock when McAuliffe strode into Middleton's headquarters. There he got startling news: the 101st was not going to Werbomont. It was on its way to Bastogne. The orders had been changed at Supreme Headquarters while McAuliffe was on the road.

The main body of the 101st got the change of order in

time. But other advance parties were still on the road, heading for Werbomont. Among these was Col. Thomas L. Sherburne, now acting commander of the 101st Artillery. Fortunately, he stopped at the same road junction as had the general, and checked for directions to Werbomont. The MP's told him that Gen. McAuliffe had come there earlier, but had gone to Bastogne, not Werbomont. Sherburne thought it best to follow the general. Moreover, he told the MP's to watch out for any other men from the 101st and to direct them to Bastogne. As a result, other officers who had left Mourmelon-le-Grand ignorant of the change in orders were redirected, and arrived before the main party.

Bastogne, a town of about 4,000, had been VIII Corps Headquarters for some time. When the German offensive began, Gen. Middleton realized at once that the town would be a prime target. It stood in the Ardennes like the hub of a giant wheel. The spokes of the wheel were seven good roads that the Germans would need for their armor, supplies, and communications. The enemy would have to make a supreme effort to seize Bastogne. Therefore, Gen. Middleton was determined to make an even more supreme effort to hold it.

At that moment, Gen. Middleton could not define precisely the extent of the German advance in front of Bastogne. But he did know the situation was precarious. "There has been a major penetration," he told McAuliffe. "Certain of my units, especially the 106th and 28th Divisions, are broken." Stragglers that came through town gave a confused picture, often exaggerated, but often terribly accurate as well, of the fighting going on to the east of Bastogne. Middleton knew there were elements of the 9th Armored Division between him and the Germans, manning roadblocks. What was left of them, or how far away the Germans were, he did not know. But they were close. Too close.

That afternoon, while the 101st was still on the road, Combat Command Bravo of the 10th Armored Division rolled into town. Its commander, Col. William L. Roberts, told Middleton he'd been ordered there to help with Bastogne's defense. Also on its way was the 705th Tank Destroyer Battalion, with its new, self-propelled 76mm guns, and the 755th Armored Field Artillery Battalion, a 155mm howitzer outfit.

Gen. Middleton immediately despatched Combat Command Bravo to the east of Bastogne, to set up roadblocks. The tanks and infantry were split into three groups, called Teams, each team bearing the code name of its CO. Thus Team Cherry, under Lt. Col. Henry T. Cherry, moved out due east about six miles to the town of Longvilly. To the northeast about the same distance, to the town of Noville, went Team Desobry. To the village of Wardin, about four miles southeast, went Team O'Hara.

Each Team leader was given the same order. He was to hold his roadblock at all costs.

From the stragglers wandering through town—the tank men without tanks, infantry without weapons, GI's separated from their chewed up units—Col. Roberts welded a reserve unit, which would feed the regular battalions as needed. This ragtag collection was nicknamed Team SNAFU. (GI slang acronym meaning Situation Normal, All Fouled Up, a phrase they regarded as applicable to everything about their Army life.)

While Combat Command Bravo moved out to the east to meet the advancing Germans, McAuliffe used the remaining hours of daylight to seek out a bivouac area for the 101st, west of Bastogne. Then Gen. Middleton phoned Gen. Omar Bradley, Commanding General, 12th Army Group, at Supreme HQ in Versailles. He told Bradley that, in his opinion, the 101st and anybody else who remained in Bastogne was doomed to be surrounded by the Germans. They might hold the town, but there was nothing all around them to stop the Germans. Encirclement was a virtual certainty.

Gen. Bradley replied, "That's okay." He wanted a stand made and Bastogne held.

The first trucks carrying the troopers began arriving in Bastogne just before midnight. The lead regiment was Col. Ewell's 501st. As the men began to de-truck, Col. Cherry arrived back in Bastogne from Longvilly for a meeting with his CO, Col. Roberts. At Longvilly he'd left his men in the charge of Capt. William F. Ryerson. It was just about at that time when the leading tanks of the *2nd Panzer Division* slipped around Longvilly and hit a column of stragglers from 9th Armored near the town of Mageret. That put the Germans just about three miles east of Bastogne, and cut off Team Cherry from the town and from its commander.

Nobody knew about this shoot-up until about two in the morning, when Col. Cherry started back to his unit. He got as far as the village of Neffe when he ran into some wounded men from 9th Armored who told him German tanks had shot up their column, which was on its way back to Bastogne. Col. Cherry radioed ahead to Capt. Ryerson in Longvilly, told him what had happened, and ordered him to send a strong patrol back toward Mageret to scout the German force. The patrol spotted three tanks and about 100 infantry, realized they couldn't fight them, and returned to Longvilly. Col. Cherry got this bad news on his radio and decided to hole up in a stone chateau just south of Neffe, along with some of his headquarters staff.

Col. Cherry was in trouble, and he knew it.

Of course he would soon have company in his troubles. Those few tanks and infantry seen by his men were just the lead elements of three German divisions converging on Bas-

togne. Aside from the *2nd Panzer Division*, there was the
elite *Panzer Lehr*, which, like the 2nd, was an armored division, and an infantry division, the *26th Volksgrenadiers*.
All together they numbered about 45,000 men, part of Baron
(General) Hasso von Manteuffel's *5th Panzer Army*.

Against these three divisions, the Screaming Eagles had
about 11,000 men, plus the artillery and antitank battalions.

On the morning of the 19th of December, Gen. Middleton
left for Neufchâteau, his new Corps HQ, twenty-five miles
from Bastogne. Gen. McAuliffe was left in charge of the
defense of Bastogne, with the order from Gen. Bradley as
transmitted by Gen. Middleton: "Hold!"

There is an old military adage that the best defense is a
good offense. As demonstrated in Holland, the senior staff
of the 101st Airborne believed in it. The way to defend
Bastogne, too, was not to sit and wait for the enemy to come
to you, not to let him pick his time and place to fight. Better
to go out and meet him and try to hit him first, and the devil
take the odds.

So Gen. McAuliffe called in Col. Ewell, pointed to a road
junction about six miles *east* of Longvilly, and told him to
take it. The presence of the *2nd Panzers* at Mageret, just
three miles outside Bastogne, was still unknown to the 101st.
At that point, because there was no unified command in the
town, Col. Roberts of the 10th Armored had not reported
the German attack to Gen. McAuliffe.

At six in the morning, the reconnaissance group set out
on the road toward Longvilly, followed by Raymond V. Bottomly, Jr., and his 1st Battalion, followed in turn by Battery
B of the 81st Airborne Antiaircraft Battalion with seven
57mm guns. The morning was dark, foggy, and cold. The
men were marching for about an hour when word came up
forward that they were on the wrong road. So they about-

faced, went back a bit, and turned down the correct fork toward Longvilly.

They approached Neffe. Here the terrain was hilly, and the road dipped and twisted along the hills rising on the left. On the right, the road dipped down to a creek. A bit of light was beginning to penetrate the fog, though visibility was still limited to about 500 yards. The troopers marched along easily, for the moment secure in the information that Combat Command Bravo was up ahead manning a roadblock.

Just outside Neffe they were taken by surprise, therefore, when a machine gun opened up on them straight down the road from the village. Major Bottomly shouted for his men to form skirmish lines, deploying them up the slopes on the left, and sending a platoon down along the bed of the creek. German tanks opened fire then. Shells exploded along the road. A hundred yards from the skirmish line, Col. Ewell found a stone house in the side of a hill and set up his command post. With him were two officers from the 907th Glider Field Artillery Battalion. Together they began to figure out where to place their artillery support. It was apparent to Col. Ewell that the 57mm guns and 1st Battalion would not be able to break the roadblock because of the tanks. At the same time, he got word from the skirmish line that the Germans were not only shooting at 1st Battalion, they were also directing fire on a chateau south of the road. Nobody knew why; this, of course, was Col. Cherry and his men.

By ten o'clock Col. Ewell decided to bring 2nd Battalion out of Bastogne to aid in the fight. Bottomly was getting nowhere. The artillery was just then beginning to fire on targets around Neffe. Bottomly had some mortars going, but the troopers could not advance. An attempt by B Company to slip around the left flank was turned back by heavy artillery and tank fire.

Lt. Thomas D. Moore, a forward observer with the Glider Artillery, decided to get up on higher ground and set up an observation post. From the crest of a hill, Moore was able to call back the German positions to his guns and soon the Glider Artillery was bringing down the houses around the German tanks and 88's.

Later that morning a runner came up to Moore's position with word that a battery of German mortars was giving 1st Battalion trouble. If he could spot the battery, the artillery could knock them out. Moore couldn't see them from his position. So he rose from cover and ran forward to get a better look. He was spotted by the Germans, but he stayed out in the open, fixed the enemy mortar positions, and phoned them back to artillery. Machine gun and tank fire flew around him, then one of the mortars sought him out. Moore wouldn't quit. He remained, adjusting the artillery fire. A mortar burst caught him and killed him, just before the Glider Artillery zeroed in and destroyed the mortars. Lt. Moore was awarded the Silver Star, posthumously.

Determined to break the German hold on the road and to take Mageret, Col. Ewell ordered 2nd Battalion to seize the little farming community of Bizory, about a mile above Neffe, on the Germans' right flank. Then he brought 3rd Battalion out of Bastogne and sent it to the village of Mont, just south of the Neffe road. His idea was to move in on Mageret from three sides, catching the enemy in a crossfire and destroying him.

At noon, Lt. Col. George M. Griswold got his 3rd Battalion on the road to Mont. At Bizory, Maj. Sammie N. Homan moved his 2nd Battalion in without opposition. On the road to Neffe, 1st Battalion was still slugging it out.

Now the 501st was ready to advance. Maj. Homan started

out on the road from Bizory to Mageret. Halfway there he ran into a unit of the *26th Volksgrenadiers,* dug in on a hill. A heavy fire fight began. Homan set up his mortars and called for artillery. Then he radioed back to Col. Ewell that he was up to his neck in Germans and could not at that moment attack Mageret itself.

South of Neffe, Col. Griswold could not advance toward Mageret either. Mont was on low ground. The Germans on the Neffe road were on high ground. Every time he tried to move his men out, the tanks of *Panzer Lehr* blasted the area with shells and machine gun fire. He did manage to slip a platoon through some woods to the chateau to help Col. Cherry, but that was all. Col. Ewell told him to hold at Mont, but to send a company a mile southeast to the village of Wardin, where they should be able to make contact with Team O'Hara of Combat Command Bravo.

It seemed to Col. Ewell then that his 501st had not accomplished much. But within the context of the entire Battle of the Bulge, he was in fact playing a key role in changing the complexion of the battle. By boldly attacking the Germans at the roadblock and engaging parts of all three German divisions converging on Bastogne, he completely confounded them. For three days they had been riding the crest of their offensive wave, forging ahead on all fronts, dealing swiftly with stubborn but scattered opposition. In front of Bastogne they had broken two American divisions and were mopping up the remnants.

Now, suddenly, they were being hit by a counterattack, obviously well-organized, backed up by strong artillery batteries. Moreover, the attackers were none other than the dreaded paratroopers with the Screaming Eagle shoulder patch. There were veterans in all three German divisions who still carried scars from their meetings with the Eagles in Normandy and Holland.

The Germans were stunned and thrown off stride, losing the momentum of their offensive. The audacious attack by one paratroop regiment made three German divisions hesitate. Yet the strategy of the entire offensive depended on precision timing, the taking of designated objectives on certain definite days. Bastogne was a vital part of that plan. The Germans had to gain control of that vital road network, and they needed it at once. Delay would doom Hitler's master stroke.

Those precious hours gained by Ewell's attack made a tremendous difference. By the time the Germans recoiled from the blow, reorganized, and prepared to advance once again, the rest of the 101st was in Bastogne and in action.

As the day wore on, the battle east of Bastogne developed and expanded, not always to the advantage of the 101st. To the southeast, Col. Griswold sent Company I of 3rd Battalion to Wardin, as ordered by Col. Ewell. The company made contact with Team O'Hara, then passed through to Wardin. There they ran into seven tanks and an entire battalion from *Panzer Lehr*. In two hours of fierce fighting the company was virtually wiped out as a fighting unit, losing forty-five men and four officers. The survivors withdrew to the woods behind Wardin and tried to make their way back to the battalion.

At the chateau, Col. Cherry's headquarters group and the platoon from 3rd Battalion were being attacked by a company of German infantry, backed up by tanks and artillery. The chateau was being blown to pieces around them. The men stayed on, the chateau blazing around them, accounting for a good many German infantry, until the smoke and the collapsing roof forced them out. They retreated to Mont.

To the northeast, where Team Desobry had been outposted at Noville, another desperate struggle was taking place. Since early morning the men of 10th Armored had been engaged with German armor. About ten-thirty in the morning, when the fog lifted, they could see that the entire countryside was covered with tanks and infantry. The two sides clashed in a violent eruption of fire and thunder. Fortunately for Team Desobry, they were backed up by a platoon from the 609th Tank Destroyer Battalion. They were knocking out the German tanks one after the other. In half an hour they destroyed ten. By noon, when the firing died down for a few moments, the battlefield was strewn with smoldering German tanks, dead tankers, and dead German infantry.

But Major Desobry realized that the morning's victory was in many respects illusory. He was outnumbered. He had beaten back a foolish frontal attack, but he knew the Germans were all around him. He could be surrounded at any moment. But he couldn't withdraw. He had been cautioned the night before by his Commanding Officer, Col. Roberts. He had been told that under no circumstances was he to retreat without permission. So he radioed his CO and asked for that permission, explaining the danger. He thought it would be best if Team Desobry moved back about a mile to the village of Foy, where he would have the advantage of high ground.

Col. Roberts pondered the request. He didn't want his men slaughtered. At the same time he knew the importance of standing firm, the need to gain time, to stall the German onslaught. He told Desobry he'd let him know, then headed for the CP of Gen. McAuliffe for a conference. On the way there he ran into Gen. Higgins, who'd flown in from London. As he was explaining the problem to Gen. Higgins, Col. Sink and Lt. Col. James L. LaPrade were passing by with the 1st Battalion of the 506th. Higgins told Sink to send

LaPrade and 1st Battalion out to Noville to give Desobry a hand, and to keep his other two battalions in ready reserve in front of Bastogne on the Noville road.

Col. Roberts then called Desobry and told him he was sending him a battalion of paratroops. Desobry replied that in that case, instead of requesting permission to withdraw, he was asking for permission to attack. Permission was granted.

When LaPrade and 1st Battalion arrived at Noville, they found the town shaking under German artillery fire. Houses and vehicles were ablaze. The situation did not look ripe for an attack. Nevertheless, the two commanders got together and agreed that an attack was necessary. The Germans controlled the high ground north and east of Noville. They had to be shoved out.

About two-thirty in the afternoon, in the face of a heavy German artillery barrage, Team Desobry and 1st Battalion of the 506th began their advance. Three tanks and armored infantry moved north. Four tanks and armored infantry moved east. LaPrade put Company B on the left flank of the armor, Company C on the right flank, and Company A in between the two armored columns.

Company C was hit just as soon as it moved out of Noville. Artillery and machine gun fire laced into the skirmish lines. A number of men fell dead, others were wounded. The troopers never stopped, firing as they pushed ahead, taking cover where they could find it, reaching the lower slopes of the ridges, climbing them, closing with the Germans.

On the left flank, about a mile away, Company B was also attacking up the slopes toward the German lines.

But in the center the attack was stopped cold. The two armored columns and Company A ran headlong into a wall of fire from 88's, tanks, and dug in machine gun emplacements. The armored columns turned around and went back to Noville. Company A tried to go on alone but it too gave up in the face of a direct fire from enemy tanks.

That left B and C Companies perched out there on their respective limbs, attacking up the snow-covered slopes without tank support. German tanks and infantry counterattacked. Some of the troopers kept climbing, and actually reached the top of the ridges, only to die there. The rest dug in on the slopes as best they could and fought it out until dark. Then what was left of the two companies slipped back to Noville.

That evening, Gen. Higgins and Col. Sink arrived for a review of the situation. The attempt to drive the Germans off the ridges had been a failure. Yet even in failure there was.an element of success. Just as the 501st had thrown the German timetable out of whack by its attack, so had the attack at Noville stalled the Germans. But the attack had shown that a unified command was necessary. LaPrade and Desobry agreed; being the ranking officer, LaPrade was given the command.

Ten minutes after Gen. Higgins and Col. Sink left Noville, their appointment of LaPrade came to naught. An 88 shell landed just outside the Command Post, killing LaPrade and seriously wounding Desobry. The young tank commander was put in an ambulance bound for Bastogne. The ambulance was captured, and Desobry was taken prisoner. Maj. Robert F. Harwick, who was Col. LaPrade's exec, took over the combined command. Maj. Charles L. Hustead took over command of the armor.

The Germans not only captured the ambulance carrying Desobry and other wounded, they took the unusual step of attacking and capturing a substantial part of the 101st's entire medical section. Normally both sides respected each other's medics. It's not known why the Germans broke this accord.

In any case, just before midnight of the 19th, a German force of tanks, half tracks, and infantry slipped around to the west of Bastogne and descended upon the 326th Medical Company. A convoy of trucks carrying wounded was just leaving. The Germans opened fire, setting the trucks ablaze. Some of the truck drivers tried to fight back, and were cut down. In fifteen minutes it was all over. A German officer came forward and demanded that Lt. Col. David Gold, the division's senior surgeon, surrender the entire medical company. Gold had no choice but to comply.

This left the 101st with a serious shortage of medics and medical supplies. Later, as the battle wore on and Bastogne was put under siege, this shortage was to be acutely felt.

At Division Command Post, Gen. Higgins, Gen. McAuliffe, and Col. Sink took a look at the situation around Noville and agreed that it could not be held. They all believed it would be better to fall back on Foy, providing a more reliable link with the other 101st regiments. But none of these officers had any control over the men from 10th Armored, and they all knew that Gen. Middleton had ordered Noville held. Accordingly, Gen. McAuliffe called Gen. Middleton, explained the tactical situation, and asked for permission to withdraw the men from Noville.

Gen. Middleton refused permission. "If we are to hold Bastogne, you cannot keep falling back," he said.

Col. Sink fretted over his men in 1st Battalion. But there was nothing he could do about it. He expressed the hope that fog during the night would keep the Germans out of Noville.

There *was* fog during the night, fog that limited the action on the Bastogne perimeter to scattered patrol action, long range mortar and artillery exchanges, and the barking of heavy machine guns, firing at ghosts in the gray mists. All night long the freezing soldiers on both sides of the lines were kept awake in their foxholes by the thump and crash and flashes of the big guns, the rattle of small arms fire. It was a night when no man dared to sleep, even if he found a few moments of peace.

The fog enabled more stragglers to sneak back into the American lines. There were tanks from the battered 9th Armored, infantry from the 28th, artillerymen, and tank destroyers. Some of the men were in such a state of shock they could no longer fight. Others absorbed themselves within 101st units and itched for revenge. Some of these men made themselves invaluable in the clashes to come.

Early on the morning of the 20th of December, all three German divisions attacked again all along the line.

From the ridge they held east of Bizory, in the center of the 101st line, 2nd Battalion of the 501st heard the clank of tank treads in the darkness. Scouts out front saw German infantry advancing across the fields. The four tank destroyers of the 705th deployed for action. In their foxholes the troopers snicked off their safeties and waited to see a target.

About seven-thirty, as the morning mist lifted, the Americans saw line after line of Germans coming towards them —it was an entire battalion from the *76th Regiment, 26th Volksgrenadiers*. Behind the infantry rolled six tanks. Maj. Homan, 2nd Battalion's commander, phoned Col. Ewell at Regiment. Ewell phoned Gen. McAuliffe at Division. In Bastogne, seven battalions of artillery had been assembled, including 75's and 105's. McAuliffe, ever the artillery officer, had gun pits dug for his howitzers so that in a few moments notice they could be swung to fire in any direction. Now, on McAuliffe's command, they swung to the east, toward Bizory.

The gray-clad German infantry advanced closer to the American lines. The tank destroyers held their fire, waiting for the enemy armor to get within range. Then, all together, in a shattering explosion of sound, both sides opened fire. The Germans swept forward, tanks spitting flame, infantry blazing away with rifles and machine pistols. The tank destroyers boomed back their answer, the troopers' machine guns swept the enemy lines. Germans fell, got up, came on again—slower this time, wavering. A German Mark IV picked off a tank destroyer, which got a direct hit on the turret, killing the gun loader. The other destroyer scored a direct hit on the Mark IV, set it afire, and killed the crew. The other two destroyers knocked out another Mark IV and a 75 mm self-propelled gun.

Homan got on the phone again to Ewell. The German infantry was bunching together. Now was the time for the howitzers. The word went back to McAuliffe. In a few minutes every artillery piece available lay down a concentrated barrage on the fields in front of 2nd Battalion. The carnage was terrible to watch. The German infantry was shredded. Those who could save themselves fled the field of battle.

In less than twenty minutes the artillery obliterated the German battalion. Troopers went down and collected the wounded and the shell-shocked.

At Noville, on the northeast perimeter, the situation was critical. All through the night the artillery of *2nd Panzer Division* had plastered the town with heavy explosive, so that hardly a building was left standing. Then, with the morning fog still heavy on the ground, the tanks came on again. German tanks and American tank destroyers duelled in half light, firing at each other's gun flashes, unable to see more than a few yards.

For two hours the battle raged on the outskirts of town. Neither side could claim an advantage. Indeed, through that thick fog, neither side could judge the effects of its firing. But the tank destroyers of the 705th were running short of armor-piercing shells, and the tanks were short on crew. Two tanks stood idle, their crews dead.

Back at Bastogne, Gen. McAuliffe was about ready to give up on Noville, notwithstanding Corps' desire to hold it. The town was undefendable on its own. It lay in a fog-shrouded hollow, facing hills swarming with German armor and artillery. Gen. McAuliffe didn't think the town could be held much longer in any case; the cost in men and armor trying to hold out for even one more day seemed a terrible waste. A defense line a bit to the southwest, near Foy, appeared to make more sense.

The actual defenders of Noville could not have agreed more. Scouting patrols had come back with reports of German armor and infantry circling around to the rear, obviously intending to cut the Bastogne road and isolate Noville. Units of the *2nd Panzer* were already attacking 3rd Battalion of the 506th at Foy.

Around noon, Gen. McAuliffe made his decision to pull out of Noville. Col. Roberts agreed that his 705th would pull out as well. At the suggestion of Col. Sink, the order went out for 3rd Battalion to counterattack at Foy. Under the umbrella of this diversion, it was hoped that the defenders at Noville could slip through the Germans and return to Bastogne. To protect the 506th counterattack, 2nd and 3rd Battalions of the 502nd would come out of reserve and move northeast to protect the left flank.

About one-thirty in the afternoon the survivors of Noville started back down the road to Foy. With them they had fifty badly wounded men in trucks and jeeps, protected by a few tanks and troopers. For once the Americans did not curse the fog. It covered their departure from Noville. The Germans on the hills did not give chase. The column moved southwest without incident until it got within half a mile of Foy. Then it ran into German armor and infantry on both sides of the road. Small arms fire broke out all along the column. The troopers and the armored infantry dashed into the woods along the road and beat off the German infantry, capturing forty. These troops were rebounding from the attack of the 506th when they happened to run into the column in the fog.

But the German armor was not so easily repulsed. Two big Mark IV's were shooting up the front of the column. They set one Sherman tank on fire, killed the driver of another. A shell knocked the turret off a third tank. The road was now blocked by wrecked tanks. The entire column was threatened with annihilation. Just then PFC. Thomas E. Gallagher, an artilleryman pressed into service on a tank destroyer, came wheeling up the road from Bastogne. Gallagher was alone on the destroyer, because the gunner had been killed and the other two crew members wounded. As he got up to the column an officer told him about the two tanks and told him to go after them. Gallagher said he needed crew. Two paratroopers of the 506th jumped on the destroyer and told Gallagher they'd help. Gallagher sent the tank destroyer forward and took on the two Mark IV's. With the help of the troopers he knocked out one of them with a direct hit. The other Mark IV turned tail and fled.

Gallagher then remained in an exposed position for the rest of the day, protecting the column as it got itself untangled and on its way again. For his bravery, Gallagher got a promotion to Corporal and the Silver Star.

Darkness was falling when the column staggered back into the lines at Bastogne. The defense of Noville had cost Team Desobry 11 tanks and its commander, wounded and taken prisoner. The 1st Battalion of the 506th lost 13 officers, including its commander, Lt. Col. LaPrade, and 199 enlisted men. But the two units had destroyed between 20 and 30 German tanks, damaged many more, and wiped out perhaps two complete battalions of German infantry.

More than that, the action at Noville had cost the Germans forty-eight hours. They could afford that even less than the loss of men and tanks.

Thus, on the 20th of December, German attacks to the east and northeast of Bastogne made little or no headway. On the southern portion of the ring closing around Bastogne, just a mile and half due south, a new threat developed that day.

Until that morning, the village of Marvie, just east of the road that runs south from Bastogne to Wiltz, was an area of relative quiet. Team O'Hara of Combat Command Bravo had a roadblock out below the village, and some engineers of the 326th Airborne put out a few mines west of the road. In the early morning hours of the 20th, Gen. McAuliffe sent 2nd Battalion of the 327th Gliders down to Marvie, to replace the engineers.

The glidermen arrived just as *Panzer Lehr* attacked Team O'Hara's roadblock half a mile south of Marvie.

An artillery concentration broke up the attack. Then the Germans put smoke around the block, indicating to the defenders that an infantry attack was imminent. While the Germans were forming up, 2nd Battalion and Team O'Hara got its men and tanks deployed. Col. O'Hara had five light tanks in Marvie itself. His heavier tanks, the Shermans, were on a hill just behind Marvie to the north. Lt. Col. Roy L. Inman, commanding 2nd Battalion, set up his CP in a building at the outskirts of the village; Company E dug in to the east, facing the Germans, with Company G on their right flank. Company F was held in reserve.

At 11:25 German guns hidden in the woods began to shell Marvie. Then four Mark IV tanks and six half-tracks carrying infantry appeared out of the woods and moved across the fields, firing as they came on. O'Hara's light tanks fired back, but their 37mm guns were useless against the Mark IV's. One light tank was blown up, another disabled. The

leader of the light tank unit wisely saw that he wasn't helping the glider troops at all; instead, he was attracting fire
from the German big guns. He asked Col. O'Hara for permission to withdraw; the permission was granted.

The German armor saw the little tanks scampering out
of town, and advanced more swiftly and boldly. As they got
closer to the village, the Shermans on the hill opened fire.
The Germans never saw them, and never knew what hit
them. One Mark IV went up in flames. Another was disabled. A half-track was blown up, killing all the infantry
inside it. Another direct hit destroyed the third Mark IV.
The last one dashed on in to Marvie, where the glidermen
knocked it out with a bazooka.

The remaining five half-tracks reached the village. The
German infantry jumped down and ducked into the houses,
firing at the glidermen. These were G Company men. They
got out of their foxholes and went into the houses after the
Germans. Within two hours thirty Germans were dead and
twenty taken prisoner. Company G lost five killed and fifteen wounded, including Col. Inman and Capt. Hugh Evans,
the company commander.

The Germans would not be getting into Bastogne via the
southern route, either.

As the afternoon light waned and snow began to fall softly
on the battlefield, Bastogne stood like a rock against the
great wave of a German Ardennes offensive. And, as a wave
breaks against a rock and flows around it, so did the German
divisions break against and flow around Bastogne. Meeting
no resistance either north or south of the Screaming Eagle
defenses, von Manteuffel's three divisions shifted to an en-
veloping maneuver around Bastogne.

On the 20th, the *2nd Panzer Division* had already split
its forces. While some were attacking at Noville and Foy,

the rest continued westward, bypassing Bastogne, heading for its principal target, the Meuse River. South of Bastogne, *26th Volksgrenadiers* and *Panzer Lehr* were also shifting the balance of their forces so that they could skirt around the defense lines and join with *2nd Panzer* behind Bastogne. Then all three divisions could once again drive for the Meuse in unison. But they still wanted and needed Bastogne itself. So von Manteuffel committed another division to its capture, the *116th Panzer Division.*

Gen. McAuliffe got the bad news about *116th Panzer* the evening of the 20th when he sped back to Corps HQ to press for supplies. He told Gen. Middleton that the Bastogne garrison was short of everything. The Corps Commander couldn't hold out much hope for resupply in the immediate future. On all sides American forces were fighting desperately to hold the Germans back from the Meuse. Deep penetrations had been made. The "bulge" was pointing menacingly toward Antwerp. Everybody had supply problems.

Then he told McAuliffe that Intelligence reported the *116th Panzer Division* coming in on Bastogne's flank. Furthermore, the only road open around Bastogne at that very moment was the road McAuliffe had traveled on to get to Corps HQ. It occurred to McAuliffe that in that case he'd better get out of there in a hurry. As he went to the door, Gen. Middleton said to him, "Now don't get yourself surrounded, Tony."

McAuliffe told his jeep driver to step on it. They raced back along the Neufchâteau road and returned to Bastogne after dark. Half an hour later, *Panzer Lehr,* by a pincer movement south of Marvie, had shut the door behind him.

Bastogne was now completely surrounded.

Chapter Eleven

General Heinrich von Luttwitz, the arrogant commander of *47th Panzer Corps,* was not his usual jaunty self on the night of December 20th. It was he who had been entrusted by von Manteuffel with the quick taking of Bastogne. It was he who had been given three crack divisions with which to do the job. And it was he who would feel the wrath of van Manteuffel, and the full fury of the *Fuhrer.* The job had not been done on schedule; the job would not be done; the job could not be done. Never mind that German Corps commanders all along the Bulge were facing similar truths. Never mind that the *Fuhrer* himself, according to High Command gossip, privately conceded that the *Wacht Am Rhein* was doomed, that the Meuse would never be crossed. The fact was that he, von Luttwitz, with all the odds in his favor, with two armored divisions and an infantry division, had been defeated by one American Airborne division and a small assortment of armor and ragtag infantry.

Defeat was the word for it. Fought to a virtual stalemate on every road to Bastogne, he now had to bypass it, let it stand there like a boil on his neck to plague him while he tried to get on with the business of reaching and crossing the Meuse. Now that he had Bastogne surrounded, he ordered Gen. Fritz Bayerlein to take *Panzer Lehr* on to

Morhet, southwest of Bastogne, leaving some men behind to help the *26th Volksgrenadiers*. North of Bastogne, Col. Meinrad von Lauchert's *2nd Panzer Division* was pointed in the direction of Marche-en Famenne, leaving enough units behind as they advanced to keep Bastogne isolated. In an arc facing Bastogne from the northeast to the southwest remained the *26th Volksgrenadiers*. Gen. Heinz Kokott, the division commander, was the only senior officer at Bastogne who still thought victory was possible. To his division went the task of investing and capturing Bastogne. He thought he and his men could do it alone, when the entire Corps had thus far failed.

Bastogne had become, as Col. Kinnard put it, "the hole in the doughnut." But this did not faze the defenders. In essence, it simplified matters. Gen. McAuliffe no longer had to be concerned with events elsewhere on the front. What mattered to him was what happened within a two-and-a-half mile radius of Bastogne. He could count on no support for the time being. The continuing heavy snowfall precluded air support or supply drops. He had to defend with what he had—and he was confident that he had enough to beat the Germans until the American forces outside the ring could counterattack and break through.

One further factor in his favor was that Gen. Middleton gave him complete command of all troops inside the Bastogne ring. From the beginning there had been divided command, although cooperation, among McAuliffe and the commanding officers of the non-Airborne units. This had to lead to a certain fragmentation of effort. But with Bastogne isolated, Gen. Middleton, as Corps Commander, called McAuliffe and gave him the reins. He also called Col. Roberts of Combat Command Bravo and explained the necessity for a unified command.

From that moment on, Roberts and McAuliffe worked as

a perfectly coordinated team. The armor and the Airborne troops meshed into a more perfectly coordinated strike force. As a result, all benefited and gained a new and healthy respect for each other; so much so that later, when the American armies regrouped for a powerful counterattack, tankers and troopers asked to remain together as a combat team.

On the morning of the 21st, a morning shrouded in freezing ground fog, as usual, Gen. Kokott sent his *77th Regiment* into action near Foy, trying to force a wedge between the 501st and the 506th positions. The *Volksgrenadiers* of the *77th* were pushing along the railroad and the railroad station at the village of Halt. The enemy advance down the track put them behind Company D of 2nd Battalion. Col. Sink was informed that a couple of enemy platoons were behind his men. In the fog, this underestimate was understandable. But it was about a battalion infiltrating, not two platoons.

Taking no chances in any case, and expecting further German attacks, Col. Sink sent A and C Companies of 1st Battalion up toward the station. When the two forces collided in the fog, a murderous fire fight began. The two sides fought at close range, visibility limited in the mist, often blazing away at the muzzle flashes winking like fireflies in the murk.

At one point during the fight squad leader Sgt. Mariano Sanchez led his men to within fifteen yards of a heavy machine gun concentration. Disregarding the deadly fire, he charged one machine gun, firing his Tommy gun from the hip. He knocked out one machine gun, then fell, mortally wounded. But inspired by his courage the rest of his squad charged the enemy. The Germans broke and ran. Eighty-five of them surrendered. Sgt. Sanchez was awarded posthumously the Silver Star for his bravery.

Lt. Anthony N. Borrelli also won a Silver Star during that same action. A platoon leader, he turned the platoon over to a sergeant and took command of the company when its commander was wounded. Then, as had Sgt. Sanchez, he charged at the enemy, firing his Tommy gun. The company, temporarily stopped, rallied behind him and renewed the assault on the *Volksgrenadiers*. Here, too, the enemy broke. Fifty of them were mowed down by Lt. Borrelli and his men, 40 taken prisoner, and another 100 pushed into the waiting troopers of the 501st, where they were either killed or captured.

That action broke the back of the *77th Volksgrenadiers*. It also pretty well destroyed its parent Division, the *26th*. Gen. Kokott was no longer sure about breaking into Bastogne on his own. As it turned out, he gave that section of the front a wide berth for a long time.

Around the rest of the circle on the 21st, the fighting was limited to patrol actions, as von Luttwitz shifted his divisions about to contain Bastogne and continue the advance to the Meuse. The German Corps Commander was also cooking up a bluff, in conspiracy with Gen. Bayerlein of *Panzer Lehr*. Little did these two German generals know that what they would hatch for their pains was to become one of the most famous legends of World War II.

At eleven-thirty on the morning of Dec. 22, four Germans (a major, a medic, captain, and two enlisted men) came marching up the road leading south from Bastogne, carrying a white flag. At his outpost in the basement of a farmhouse, Sgt. Oswald Butler of 2nd Battalion, 327th Gliders, spotted the men and phoned back to the Command Post. "Four Krauts coming up the road," he said. "They're carrying a white flag. Maybe they want to surrender."

Then Butler, along with Sgt. Carl Dickinson of 2nd Battalion and PFC. Ernest D. Premetz, a medic who spoke German, went out on the road to meet the four Germans. The German captain could speak English, and he said to them,

"We are parlementaries. We want to speak to your commanding general."

The Germans were taken to the platoon leader, Lt. Leslie E. Smith. The lieutenant left the two enlisted men under guard, then blindfolded the two officers and took them to the CP of his company commander, Capt. James F. Adams. The captain called Battalion, and word was relayed all the way back to Division that Germans had come in with surrender terms.

The rumor quickly spread around the southern perimeter that the Germans wanted to surrender. The sector was certainly quiet. Men rose from their foxholes and walked around, visiting with buddies. Others took time out to shave for the first time in days, or wash with melted snow.

But, like most GI rumors, this one was wrong. It was the Germans who wanted *them* to surrender.

By this time Maj. Alvin Jones, at Regiment, had received from the German officers a written ultimatum from Gen. von Luttwitz, one copy in German, one with an English translation. Jones got Col. Harper, the Regimental Commander, and together they went to the operations room at Division HQ, where they found Gen. McAuliffe and his staff, waiting for the message.

Col. Ned Moore, acting as Chief of Staff, took the typewritten message and scanned the English translation.

"What's it say, Ned?" asked McAuliffe.

"They want you to surrender," replied Moore.

"Aw, nuts!" exclaimed McAuliffe, laughing.

Here is the exact text of the German ultimatum:

December 22nd 1944

To the U.S.A. Commander of the encircled town of Bastogne.

The fortune of war is changing. This time the U.S.A.

forces in and near Bastogne have been encircled by strong German armored units. More German armored units have crossed the River Ourthe near Ortheuville, have taken Marche and reached St. Hubert by passing through Hompre-Sibret-Tillet. Libramont is in German hands.

There is only one possibility to save the encircled U.S.A. troops from total annihilation: that is the honorable surrender of the encircled town. In order to think it over a term of two hours will be granted beginning with the presentation of this note.

If this proposal should be rejected one German Artillery Corps and six heavy A.A. Battalions are ready to annihilate the U.S.A. troops in and near Bastogne. The order for firing will be given immediately after this two hours' term.

All the serious civilian losses caused by this artillery fire would not correspond with the well known American humanity.

The German Commander

Gen. McAuliffe's laughter was genuine derision. He thought von Luttwitz was way out of line. His men had been giving the Germans a good beating. Morale was good. He took up a pencil and began to think of an answer. After a few minutes he said to his staff, "Well, I don't know what to tell them."

Col. Kinnard then said, "Well, General, that first remark of yours would be hard to beat."

Gen. McAuliffe didn't understand what Kinnard meant. Kinnard repeated it. "You said, 'Nuts!' "

The staff laughed and applauded. Gen. McAuliffe nodded his head. "That's it," he said. Taking up the pencil, he wrote:

To the German Commander:
  Nuts!
From the American Commander

McAuliffe then gave the piece of paper to Col. Harper and asked him to see that it was delivered.

"I'll deliver it myself," said Harper. "It'll be a lot of fun."

Col. Harper went back to the two German officers at the command post. "I have the American Commander's reply," he said.

"Is it written or verbal?" asked the German captain.

"It is written." Harper stuck the paper into the hand of the captain, who was still blindfolded. "The answer is 'Nuts!' " he said.

The captain could only translate this literally into German for the major. *"Er sagt Niessen,"* he said. Of course neither enemy officer understood. "Is the reply negative or affirmative?" the captain asked. "If it is the latter I will negotiate further."

Col. Harper was losing patience with the Germans' arrogant manner. "The reply is definitely not affirmative," he said angrily. He then took the Germans back to the outpost where the two enlisted men waited with the white flag. He removed the blindfolds, and said to the captain, "If you don't understand what 'Nuts!' means, in plain English it's the same as 'Go to Hell.' And I'll tell you something else. If you continue to attack we will kill every goddam German that tries to break into this city!"

The German officers stood stiffly to attention and saluted. "We will kill many Americans," the captain said. "This is war."

"On your way, Bud," Col. Harper said.

The delivery of the ultimatum and the legendary reply of

Gen. McAuliffe consumed perhaps half an hour. Thus, according to the message, the threatened German bombardment would start between one-thirty and two. It never came. The front remained quiet until four o'clock when about fifty German infantryman made an attack against the outposts of Company F, 327th Gliders, over the same road traveled by the German messengers several hours earlier. Lt. Smith and Sgts. Butler and Dickinson had the pleasure of punctuating their Commanding General's reply with bullets as the Germans advanced. The attack faded away. Another attack an hour later against the same spot met the same fate.

That was it for the day. Gen McAuliffe had called von Luttwitz's bluff and the German Commander could but show a very weak hand indeed.

The optimism of Gen. McAuliffe was not without reservation, however. While he felt strong enough to dare Luttwitz to show his hand, he knew he was acting on the assumption that help for Bastogne was just around the corner. He had been promised that help, and he needed it badly. Supplies were very low. Small arms ammunition was being scrounged from the bodies of the dead and wounded. Artillery shells were being rationed. Most of the batteries were down to ten rounds per gun. Frustrated artillerymen got reports of beautiful targets time and time again—a group of tanks, or bunched infantry—but they could not fire.

At one point, asked for special permission to fire a barrage, McAuliffe replied, "If you see 400 Germans in a 100-yard area, and they have their heads up, you can fire artillery at them—but not more than two rounds."

Food, warm clothes, blankets, medical supplies—all were needed desperately. Winter had come to the Ardennes in earnest. Temperatures dropped to below freezing. Many of the Screaming Eagles, departing Mourmelon-le-Grand on short notice, had not drawn winter clothing. Cases of trench foot and frostbite filled the hospital, though these men, reluctant to leave the fighting, had to be ordered off the line.

At the makeshift Bastogne hospital, set up in an old Belgian Army garage, the loss of the medical unit to the Germans was sorely felt. The wounded were laid out on sawdust covered with blankets. There were no beds. There was no heat. The only hot food was coffee and pancakes made from flour found in a storehouse.

The medics were short of everything—plasma, dressings, morphine, and, most of all, personnel. Many wounded died because it was impossible to give them proper care. Many more died when German bombers came over one night and dropped incendiaries. One hit a collecting point for wounded and killed them all. A volunteer Belgian nurse was also killed in the raid.

So McAuliffe had reservations about the ability of the Bastogne defenders to hold out more than a few more days. On the 22nd, the day he'd scornfully rejected the surrender ultimatum, he'd been promised an airlift of supplies. The weather cancelled it out. He'd also been told by Gen. Middleton that the 4th Armored Division of Gen. George Patton's Third Army was on its way from the southwest. This was true, but Patton's tankers had to fight their way through a horde of Germans before they could reach Bastogne.

To hang on, the Screaming Eagles needed a break—especially a break in the weather.

They got it on the 23rd, like the delivery of an early Christmas present.

The morning dawned bitter cold, barely above zero, but the sun rose, dispelled the fog and the mist, and turned the snow into dazzling white crystals. GI's huddled together in their foxholes, turned their eyes skyward in hope. At first there was nothing, just the silence of winter. Then, about nine o'clock, the droning sounds of aircraft engines could be heard—American aircraft.

A small flight of C-47's appeared. Then from their bellies men tumbled, white parachutes opened, and down to earth came the members of the Pathfinder team who would lead in the supply planes.

An hour later sixteen C-47's came droning over. Now the German ack-ack opened up. Dirty brown puffs of smoke exploded amongst the fat-bellied transports. A couple were hit and fell, trailing smoke. But the rest stayed in formation and dropped their bundles. Parachutes in brilliant red, yellow, and blue, color-coded for identification, billowed in the freezing currents of air. The supply bundles dropped squarely on target.

On the ground men came up out of their foxholes and dared a sniper bullet to wave and cheer at the planes as they circled over the drop zone.

All day long the airdrop continued. Supply crews on the ground raced from the drop zone directly to the front line units, breaking open ammo boxes and ration cartons as they drove, aware of the precious nature of their cargo. By four o'clock 241 planes had dropped 144 tons of supplies on the drop zone. On the next day another 100 tons was dropped. The supply situation changed from hazardous to merely critical.

But the clear weather brought out more than just the C-47 transports. As the supply planes shuttled back and forth that morning, out of the clear blue sky plummetted a flight of P-47's. They dropped low over Bastogne and zoomed off to the northwest, catching a German armored column by complete surprise. Not an antiaircraft gun fired at them as they bombed and strafed the column. Trucks and tanks went up in flames. The infantry ran for the woods. Some made it to safety; many others fell in the snow, riddled by .50 caliber machine gun bullets.

The P-47's had a field day. Finding targets was easy. Vehicle tracks in the snow led them to transport parking areas and heavy gun and tank concentrations. The planes came in low over the woods, bombing and strafing the German positions. The *Luftwaffe* was nowhere to be seen. Plumes of black smoke rose in a large arc around Bastogne where the fighter bombers did their work.

In effect, the crisis was over.

Not the fighting, however. There was more of that to come—more fierce, and more costly than all the fighting to date around Bastogne. But the fortunes of the 101st and the other units trapped in Bastogne took a turn for the better with the clearing of the skies on December 23rd. The next day the supply drops and the air assaults by the P-47's continued. On the ground, the fighting was limited to patrol actions.

On Christmas Eve, Gen. McAuliffe spoke to Gen. Middleton on the phone. "The finest Christmas present the 101st could get," McAuliffe said, "would be a relief tomorrow."

It was on its way. Since six o'clock in the morning of December 22, the Combat Commands of the 4th Armored Division had been fighting their way toward Bastogne. The advance, through the German *5th Parachute Division,* was costing heavily in tanks and troops. On Christmas Day, 4th Armored was still too many miles southwest of Bastogne to play Santa for the battered battalions of Bastogne.

Christmas Day meant something to the Germans, too. Twice on Christmas Eve the *Luftwaffe* bombed Bastogne. Von Luttwitz thought it might be nice to give the city to Hitler for a Christmas present. Following the second air raid, he sent the *77th Regiment* and a strong armored force into an all-out attack against the 101st perimeter near Longchamps, northwest of Bastogne.

It began with an artillery barrage at two-forty-five in the morning. Here the perimeter was held by the 502nd and

1st and 3rd Battalions of the 327th Gliders. The troopers and the glidermen woke up and went to their guns. In more than one case men in foxholes together shook hands, certain they would never see another Christmas.

After the artillery barrage.came the German tanks (Mark IV's), German infantry riding them, firing their rifles. Quickly the tanks broke through the American outposts, overran the first line of foxholes, shot up command posts, and destroyed communications.

The troopers and the glidermen did not panic. They ducked down in their foxholes and let the tanks ride past them, over them. Then they rose again and picked off the German infantry. Machine guns and bazookas roared into action. The German grenadiers were sent spinning off the tanks into the snow.

Five Mark IV's made a run at a platoon of troopers. With the troopers were a squad of Airborne Engineers. Six enlisted men of the engineers, all privates, volunteered to try to put flanking fire on the tanks and turn them away from the endangered platoon. Armed only with M1 rifles and a rocket launcher, the six men ran out over open terrain, dodging mortar and bullet fire, and took on the five tanks, loaded with German infantry.

Incredibly, the six men turned the tanks toward them, and away from the platoon. And, as the tanks turned and headed for the flank, they lined up perfectly for two tank destroyers hidden in a wood nearby. Three tanks were knocked out with the first volley. A bazooka round got the fourth. The rocket launcher the fifth. The German grenadiers left alive meekly surrendered.

The six Engineer privates all received the Silver Star. They were: Pvt. Joe J. Berra, Pvt. Joe H. Douglas, Pvt. Jacques I. Levan, Pvt. Cort L. Paine, Pvt. Homer L. Williams, and Pvt. Stanley W. Wieczorek.

On the 327th's front eighteen tanks attacked the lines, also laden with infantry. After their initial breakthrough, this German force ran headlong into a curtain of fire. The 327th had eight tank destroyers, two Sherman tanks, and a battery of artillery in support, all now well-supplied with shells.

As the Mark IV's broke into the open and made a run for the village of Hemroulle, just outside Bastogne, every American gun in the area opened up. The fire was so intense and so concentrated it was impossible to tell whose guns were knocking out which tanks. The Mark IV's were blasted into piles of junk. The infantry riding them were cut to ribbons. Not one tank escaped. Not one German soldier.

Later, it was learned that Gen. von Manteuffel himself had come down from Army HQ to order this Christmas Day attack. He brought with him the crack *15th Panzergrenadier Division,* and it was the armor from this unit which had aided the *77th.* He also came with orders that Bastogne had to be taken at all costs on Christmas Day. In fact, German troops had to be in Bastogne by eight in the morning, before the dreaded P-47's could be brought out against them.

Long before the deadline, Gen. Kokott of the *26th Volksgrenadiers* knew all was lost. He asked for permission to withdraw. Permission was refused. He continued the battle well into the day, knowing full well he was accomplishing nothing but the killing of more men.

That night, Gen. McAuliffe called Gen. Middleton again and expressed his disappointment that no relief column had arrived. He felt let down. On the other side of the lines, the German generals were feverishly concocting new excuses to give Hitler for their continued failure to take Bastogne.

It was not a very merry Christmas all around.

Chapter Twelve

It was three o'clock on the afternoon of December 26. On a hill overlooking the village of Clochimont stood Lt. Col. Creighton W. Abrams, commander of the 37th Tank Battalion, and Lt. Col. George L. Jacques, commander of the 53rd Armored Infantry Battalion. These two units, together with three battalions of 105mm and one battery of 155mm howitzers, comprised Combat Command R of the 4th Armored Division. Four miles northeast of Clochimont lay Bastogne.

The mission of Combat Command R was to swing northwest toward the highway into Bastogne near Sibret, on their way toward breaking through the German ring. Their drive northward had cost Combat Command R heavily; Abrams was down to 20 medium tanks and Jacques had lost 230 men. Now, as they prepared to attack toward Sibret, from their hill they saw a flight of C-47 transports winging over Bastogne, flying straight and true through the deadly brown puffs of ack-ack.

Something about the sight moved the two officers. Somehow it symbolized the heroic struggle that had been going on inside Bastogne for ten days. Both men felt a surge of pride in being part of an army that could boast of such men.

Both men felt that no more time was to be wasted, that attacking the heavily defended village of Sibret would delay them still further, whittle away yet more at their depleted forces.

Between them, they agreed to send a strike force due north to the village of Assenois and straight on through to Bastogne. Abrams ordered his Operations Officer, Capt. William A. Dwight, to take a light force of tanks and infantry, hit Assenois, and keep on going until he reached the Bastogne perimeter. The artillery would stand in place and precede the strike force with a barrage.

Lt. Charles B. Boggess, in the lead tank, called down the artillery as he approached Assenois. The big guns plastered the town and the woods behind it. Shells were still falling as the strike force entered Assenois. The Germans in the houses opened fire. The infantry with the strike force jumped down from the tanks and the half-tracks and returned the enemy fire. But five tanks and one half-track charged right through the town and out the other end. Three of the tanks got a couple of hundred yards ahead of the others. Quickly some Germans ran out of the houses and mined the road behind them. The half-track hit a mine and blew up. Capt. Dwight jumped out of his tank and with some of his men began to clear the mines, covered by the other tank and some infantry.

Lt. Boggess and the other two tankers kept on going. About 4:45 Lt. Boggess spotted some men in foxholes wearing American helmets. He raised the turret hatch of his tank, looked out, and called to the men. Nobody in the foxholes moved. These troopers of the 326th Engineers had heard too many stories of Germans riding around in captured American tanks speaking perfect English.

Lt. Boggess called out again. "It's okay. We're from the Fourth Armored!"

Lt. Duane J. Webster rose from his foxhole and approached the tank, keeping Boggess covered with his carbine. "I'm Lt. Webster," he said warily. "You guys got any water?"

The siege of Bastogne was broken.

Half an hour later Capt. Dwight arrived with the rest of the strike force. He radioed back for Col. Abrams to bring on the rest of Combat Command R. The tanks and infantry moved forward, clearing Assenois and widening the corridor as they came. By eight that evening, Combat Command R arrived in Bastogne with a bag of 428 prisoners.

With Abrams was Gen. Taylor, who had flown back from the United States as soon as the 101st was called back into action. By the time he'd arrived at the front, Bastogne had been surrounded and he'd attached himself to Patton's forces to be on hand for the breakthrough.

With the relief of Bastogne came the end of the Germans' grandiose plans for the Ardennes offensive. Hitler may not have thought so, but his generals did. The *Fuhrer* came up with a new plan, called *Nordwind* (Northwind), which he said would knock the Western Allies out of the war. He dreamed still of a negotiated settlement with America, England, and Canada that would leave him free to take on the Russians with a one-front war. But while his High Command paid lip service to his orders, in actual fact it decided that the only sensible thing to do was consolidate the gains made and regroup the overextended divisions.

The capture of Bastogne was perhaps more important than ever now. Instead of a base for the offensive push at the southern edge of the Bulge, it was seen as a vital hub of a new defensive network. In American hands it was a dagger stuck in the left flank of the German armies.

For a few days both sides seemed to pause for a rest. Another calm before a looming storm. Supplies and men poured through the Assenois corridor into Bastogne. The wounded were taken out. Prisoners shipped to the rear.

Tributes to the defenders of Bastogne came from all sides. Congratulations arrived from the Canadian Army and the British Army, from generals Patton and Middleton, from the Allied High Command.

Perhaps most trenchant of all, a tribute nobody knew about till after the war. Captured documents revealed that at the height of the siege, Hitler turned to his staff and said about Gen. McAuliffe and the men of Bastogne, "I would like to see the German general who would fight on with the same stubborn tough resistance in a situation which seemed just as hopeless."

On the 29th of December, the first rumblings of an impending big battle were heard. Patrols along the perimeter brought back word of something doing behind the German lines. Air reconnaissance and fighter planes reported a buildup of German armor. The woods around Bastogne were filled with infantry. It looked as though the Germans were getting ready for a new assault on Bastogne.

They were indeed, and with more men, more armor, and greater fury than ever before. Four fresh German divisions were diverted to the Bastogne area. The elite *Fuhrer Escort Brigade* was ordered to attack the newly opened corridor, slam it shut, and once again isolate Bastogne. At the same time, the *1st, 9th,* and *12th SS Panzer* divisions would attack in an arc from the northwest to the southeast. The city would be pulverized and the defenders destroyed.

On the morning of December 30, both sides leaped at each other's throats simultaneously. By coincidence, the renewed German attack and the beginning of a great American counteroffensive jumped off at almost precisely the same hour. Southwest of Bastogne the U.S. 11th Armored and the 87th

Infantry divisions swung into action. Northeast of Bastogne it was the 26th and 35th Infantry divisions. They ran smack into four panzer divisions, two infantry and a parachute division and the *Fuhrer Escort Brigade.*

For the next two days the fighting raged furiously all around Bastogne. For the most part, the 101st perimeter was relatively quiet, with the long-range artillery getting most of the work in support of the wide-ranging battles. On New Year's Eve, the Screaming Eagles welcomed in 1945 with a tremendous barrage. Every artillery piece, tank cannon, and mortar hurled at least one shell into the German positions at all points along the perimeter.

The snows were falling again in the Ardennes. The weather was brutally cold; the roads were like ice rinks. Not conditions conducive to the movement of men and armor, but still both sides poured more and more into the terrible meat grinder of the Ardennes battlefield.

On January 3 the Screaming Eagles were ordered into the battle, and given the word to switch from defense to offense. They were to attack northeast out of Bastogne and clear the Bois Jacques (woods) around Foy. Then it would be on to Noville. At noon 2nd and 3rd Battalions of the 501st began the advance. The left flank of the advance was held by troopers of the 506th; the right flank by a battalion from the 6th Armored Division.

The conditions in the woods were terrible, much more suited to defense than offense. The snow was chest deep in some places. The Germans were well dug in, foxholes and machine gun nests well camouflaged. In the gloom of the forest, contact between units was difficult; often entire squads became lost and wandered off to fight alone. Into this frozen wasteland of darkness and death the two battalions of Geronimos advanced, made contact, and swiftly became embroiled in a savage struggle.

At first the troopers met with some success. But when battalions advance, they expose flanks to counterattacks. In this instance, the men of the 6th Armored were to have advanced on the right along with the troopers to protect that flank, but, meeting a strong force of German tanks and infantry, they dropped back. Into the vacuum charged the Germans. Quickly the reserve company of 2nd Battalion, Company E, was brought up into position facing the German counterblow.

The enemy came across the fields bunched up in company formation, much to the pleasant surprise of the Company E troopers. When the infantry got in range, the troopers opened fire. The advance echelons of the Germans disappeared under the hail of small arms fire. Undaunted however, the Germans swung around for a left hook at the troopers. As they did so, their strength was revealed to be enormous— more than a battalion of infantry, at least four tanks, and six half-tracks.

This was more than Company E could handle. Word was sent to Battalion Commander Sammie Homan, who radioed for armor. He was told Team O'Hara would be coming. Before the armor arrived, the right flank of the American battalions started getting a pounding as they had never gotten before. Artillery, mortars, tank cannon, Screaming Meemies, machine guns, and small arms fire poured into the troopers. What they had run into, of course, was a large force of two *Panzergrenadier* divisions bent on taking Bastogne, moving up over that same route. The two advancing units bumped head-on in the Bois Jacques.

That was not all. While the 501st was battling for its life in the woods, several miles to the west the 502nd was set upon by elements of two more *Panzergrenadier* divisions. For two days a battle raged over this sector of the perimeter that many Screaming Eagle officers considered the most terrible of the war. At one point in the Bois Jacques the slaughter on both sides became so ghastly that even the medics were being shot down. Finally a short truce was agreed upon to move out the wounded; then the battle was resumed. The fighting was brutal, personal; it had to be in those dark and ghostly woods. Often it came down to the knife and the pistol—and even bare hands. Later, a German soldier and a paratrooper would be found dead in the snow, side by side, blue marks on their throats the only signs of their struggle. They had throttled each other to death.

On the 502nd front the fighting was equally fierce, almost tragically heroic. The Germans attacking here had so much armor they were able to send individual tanks against lone troopers. Sometimes a tank would settle over a foxhole and run its motor till the exhaust fumes asphyxiated the helpless GI.

The troopers more than took it. They gave it back. They stood fast against the tanks and picked off the German infantry riding the armor or advancing behind it. But casualties were awful. Half of the second battalion was wiped out. Men with bazookas fought the tanks until their rockets ran out, then they picked up carbines and fought the infantry. Nobody moved backward one foot.

Gen. Taylor threw in all the reserves he could spare. Team Cherry of the 10th Armored rushed in to help with its tank destroyers. Engineers from the 326th picked up bazookas and rifles, and laid mines under the noses of the tank cannons. As the hours flew by, Col. Chappuis, 2nd Battalion's Commander, could still report to Division, "Situation under control."

On the night of the first day of this bloodiest of battles, the Screaming Eagles got a break. In the darkness a German soldier stumbled into the American lines, hopelessly lost. He asked an American soldier for directions, thinking he was within his own lines. Taken prisoner and questioned, it turned out he was a messenger, and, talking freely, he told of a big new attack scheduled for the next morning by the *15th SS Panzergrenadier Division,* against the positions of the 327th Gliders.

Acting upon this information a tremendous artillery barrage was put on the area pinpointed by the captured German as the Germans' jump-off point. That this barrage did a tremendous amount of damage was not learned till later, from prisoners. To the men in the foxholes on the front line it seemed to make little difference. In the cold light of dawn the Germans attacked just the same, advancing with a large force of tanks and infantry.

Forewarned, at least, the glidermen were ready. Their flank rested on the flank of the 502nd, and it was across this broad front that the battle continued through the second day. The momentum of the Germans' first charge carried several tanks and a few hundred grenadiers through the 327th positions and on into the village of Longchamps. Some got to within a hundred yards of the 1st Battalion Command Post. To the rescue came 1st Battalion of the 502nd, which had been in regimental reserve. The troopers knocked out the tanks and sent the grenadiers reeling back to their own lines.

And suddenly, quiet settled over the battlefields. The Germans melted back into the depths of the woods of Bois Jacques and into their original positions north and northwest of the Bastogne perimeter. Behind them, they left the charred hulks of tanks and half-tracks by the dozen, black blots in the snow, and the lifeless bodies of the grenadiers, hundreds of them, already stiffening grotesquely in the near zero cold.

From January 5 to January 8 the quiet held. While other

American divisions continued the counteroffensive aimed at liquidating the bulge, the 101st remained in place, awaiting the word to continue the advance toward Noville. As for the Germans, official U.S. Intelligence reports had them "licking their wounds" after the two-day battle, content to hold their positions.

By the 9th of January, the big American push had straightened out a substantial portion of the bulge. North and south of Bastogne two great American armies were ready to launch the last part of the counteroffensive. The Screaming Eagles, part of the Third Army, got their orders: "Prepare to attack on Corps orders to capture Noville and maintain contact with the 6th Armored Division and the 17th Airborne Division."

On a dull gray morning the 101st advanced through falling snow along the road to Noville, the 506th leading the way. The roads were slippery, the woods treacherous, the enemy vicious and tenacious. But now the tide had turned. The men felt it. They were fighting a beaten army trying to preserve what it could. Prisoners were taken in batches of platoon size, sometimes company size, prisoners no longer arrogant and confident, but dispirited and void of hope.

Yet the advance was not easy. Day by day the casualties mounted. One of these was Col. Ewell, wounded in the foot and forced out of action, his combat career over. His place as regimental commander of the 501st was taken by Lt. Col. Ballard. Major Shettle (promoted from Captain) was another casualty, hit by shrapnel. Every regiment suffered, every company, every squad. In some platoons hardly a dozen men could say they knew each other since their training jumps in the states. Replacements came in regularly to fill the gaps; some lived a day, some a week, some came through unscathed.

Then Lt. Col. Stopka was killed. This was on the 14th, the sixth day of the advance. Just a few days earlier Col. Stopka had actually received the Distinguished Service Cross awarded him when he helped Col. Cole in the bayonet charge at Carentan. Now both men were dead.

The next day, 2nd Battalion of the 506th attacked and took Noville. On the 16th men of the 101st advanced beyond the town and dug in on the high ground east of it. There was one more day's fighting, as men of the 502nd cleared Bourcy, east of Noville, and took the high ground above it.

Then the Screaming Eagles stopped. Word came down from Corps that the Division was to be relieved and rested in reserve. The 11th Armored Division was coming up to take its place in the front lines.

In the battered town square of Bastogne on the 18th of January, 500 men representing the various units of the 101st stood for a ceremony. Gen. Middleton, the Corps Commander, presented Silver Star medals to Maj. John D. Hanlon of the 502nd, Lt. Frank R. Stanfield of the 506th, and Staff Sgt. Lawrence F. Casper and Pvt. William J. Wolfe of the 327th.

Then Gen. Middleton said, "From personal acquaintance with your gallant fight at Carentan, knowledge of your deeds in Holland, and now, here in Bastogne, I think you're the best bunch of fighting men in the United States or any other army in the world!"

For the Screaming Eagles, the battle of Bastogne was the climactic battle of the war. Similarly, the Battle of the Ardennes, of which Bastogne was a vital part, was the last great battle of the European war. When Hitler's last offensive—his final gamble—failed to pay off, it was clear to all but a few blind Nazi fanatics that the days of the Third Reich were numbered. A saner mind than Hitler's would have surrendered after the Battle of the Ardennes and saved much bloodshed and much destruction. But he swore he would fight to the end, and in the end he made a junk heap of most of Germany, burying himself, a suicide, in the ashes of a ruined Berlin, his capital city.

So, because Hitler would not surrender, though beaten, a few more thousand American soldiers died or were maimed. Some of them were Screaming Eagles. A week after being relieved at Bastogne, the 101st was given a quiet four-mile front to maintain along the Moder River, in Alsace, on the German border. The 501st and the 327th went into the line, taking over from the 42nd Division, while the 502nd and 506th went into reserve.

To a man in a foxhole, there is of course no such thing as security, no front line that is safe. He lives with the awareness that at any given second a bullet or a piece of shrapnel can kill or cripple him. But he can make comparisons, and, in comparison, the month spent on the line in Alsace was a quiet one for the 101st. Action was limited to patrols. The men were now better equipped, better fed. Some were billetted in houses. Hot food was more frequent. Passes were issued. There were portable showers, even movies like "Rhapsody in Blue," "Buffalo Bill," "Mrs. Parkington."

In that quiet month on the line in Alsace, 31 men were killed, 168 wounded.

At the end of February the 101st returned to Mourmelon-le-Grand for a complete rest. There, in a remarkable ceremony on March 15, Gen. Eisenhower awarded the 101st the Distinguished Unit Citation, the first time in the history of the United States Army that an entire division was so honored.

Said Gen. Eisenhower:

It is a great personal honor for me to be here today to take part in a ceremony that is unique in American history. Never before has a full division been cited by the War Department in the name of the President for gallantry in action. This day marks the beginning of a new tradition in the American Army. With that tradition, therefore, will always be associated the name of the 101st Airborne Division and of Bastogne.

. . . it is entirely fitting and appropriate that you should be cited for that particular battle. It happened to be one of those occasions when the position itself was of the utmost importance to the Allied Forces. You, in reserve, were hurried forward and told to hold that position. All the elements of drama, of battle drama, were there. You were cut off, you were surrounded. Only valor, complete self-confidence in yourselves and in your leaders, a knowledge that you were well trained, only the determination to win, could sustain soldiers under those conditions. You were given a marvelous opportunity, and you met every test.

. . . it is my great privilege to say to you here today, to the 101st Division and all its attached units, "I am awfully proud of you."

. . . Good luck and God be with each of you.

Epilogue

At Mourmelon-le-Grand, training began for Operation Eclipse, aptly named, for it was supposed to be part of the final blow against Germany. Under Eclipse, the 101st, the 82nd, and British airborne divisions were to drop on Berlin, make contact with the Russians, and finish off Hitler. For many reasons, mostly political, Operation Eclipse was cancelled. Instead, the Division was ordered to the Ruhr, the industrial heart of Germany, where they went into the line near Dusseldorf. The 501st remained behind at Mourmelon-le-Grand, preparing for a special mission, a drop on prisoner-of-war camps. This, too, never came off, and the 501st joined the Division at Berchtesgaden after V-E Day.

The Division's time in the Ruhr was even better than the Alsace assignment. The consensus was "We never had it so good." The men were quartered in the German houses. Mail arrived regularly. USO shows made the rounds. There was a minimum of patrolling across the Rhine. The war was rapidly coming to an end. Few German soldiers wanted to die in those last few weeks, and many patrols picked up prisoners eager to surrender.

With the collapse of the area known as The Ruhr Pocket, the Division was shifted again, this time to the mountainous area of the south, in Bavaria, called the Redoubt. This order was met with something less than joy by the troopers. It was expected that the last few die-hard fanatics among the Nazis and the SS troops would make a last stand here. The area was ideally suited to defense, being so mountainous, with narrow roadways where a squad could hold up a regiment. Nobody in the Division looked forward to rooting out any Germans holed up in the Redoubt.

When they got to Bavaria, the troopers were pleasantly surprised to find the Redoubt virtually undefended. Such resistance as they met was usually token. The Germans would fire a few harmless shots, or blow a bridge, and then surrender. There was no longer any order in the German Army. Surrenders came by the regiment, by the division.

The last real combat mission for the 101st in World War II·was the capturing of Berchtesgaden, Hitler's vacation retreat high in the mountains. The area was supposed to be full of Nazi bigwigs and loot taken from occupied countries. The troopers met no resistance in Berchtesgaden. They accepted the surrender of two entire German Army Corps, the *XIIIth SS and the LXXXIInd*. Then they went looking for Nazi bigwigs. The men of the 506th found Field Marshall Albert Kesselring, Commander-in-Chief of the German Armies, sitting in his private nine-car train. Kesselring agreed to surrender only to Gen. Taylor. Then Dr. Robert Ley, the notorious leader of the Nazi Labor Front, was captured. Other prominent Nazis captured were Franz Xavier Schwarz, Julius Streicher (later hanged for his war crimes), and "The Butcher of Paris," *Obergruppenfuhrer* (Lt. General) Karl Albrecht Oberg, Chief of the SS in France. The German tank wizard, Gen. Heinz Guderian, was also captured, in nearby Stuhlfelden, by troopers of 3rd Battalion, the 506th.

The 101st also uncovered an incredible amount of stolen treasure at Berchtesgaden—paintings, sculptures, gold and silver artifacts, jewels. Much of this loot was stolen from museums all over Europe by Hermann Goering.

The treasure trove was given an estimated value at anywhere from two hundred to five hundred million dollars.

The war in Europe officially came to an end on May 8, 1945. The 101st stayed on at Berchtesgaden until August 1, when it was relieved by the 42nd Division and moved to a new camp at Auxerre, France. There it began training anew for operations against Japan. When Japan surrendered in August, the 101st Division was deactivated, and the men sent home.

On November 30, 1945, in Auxerre, Col. Kinnard wrote the Division's last daily bulletin. He wrote:

To those of you left to read this last daily bulletin—do not dwell on the disintegration of our great unit, but rather be proud that you are of the "old guard" of the greatest division ever to fight for our country. Carry with you the memory of its greatness wherever you go, being always assured of respect when you say, "I served with the 101st."

Today, reactivated and reorganized as an Air Assault Division using helicopters instead of parachutes, the 101st is based at Ft. Campbell, Kentucky.

Bibliography

Blumenson, Martin. *U.S. Army in World War II: Breakout and Pursuit*. Washington, D.C., Office of the Chief of Military History, 1961.

Bradley, General Omar N. *A Soldier's Story*. New York: Henry Holt, 1951.

Burgett, Donald. *Currahee*. London: Hutchinson & Co., 1967.

Cole, H.M. *The Ardennes: The Battle of the Bulge*. Washington, D.C., Office of the Chief of Military History, 1961.

Guderian, General Heinz. *Panzer Leader*. New York: E. P. Dutton, 1962.

Harrison, Gordon A. *Cross-Channel Attack*. Washington, D.C., Office of the Chief of Military History, 1951.

Koskimaki, George E. *D-Day With the Screaming Eagles*. New York: Vantage Press, 1970.

Mackenzie, Fred. *The Men of Bastogne*. New York: David McKay, 1968.

Merriam, Robert E. *Dark December*. New York: Ziff-Davis, 1947.

Nobecourt, Jacques. *Hitler's Last Gamble: The Battle of the Bulge*. New York: Schocken Books, 1967.

Rapport, Leonard, and Northwood, Arthur J. *Rendezvous with Destiny: A History of the 101st Airborne Division*. Washington, D.C.: Infantry Journal Press, 1948.

Urquhart, Maj. Gen. R.E. *Arnhem*. New York: W. W. Norton, 1958.

Index

About the Author

Milton J. Shapiro was born and raised in Brooklyn, New York. He went to Boys High School there, and then to the College of the City of New York. Two years in the Army, including a year with the 13th Air Force in the Philippines, interrupted his college education. Resuming at CCNY, Mr. Shapiro was graduated with a BBA and served as Features Editor of *Ticker,* the college newspaper. While still a senior at CCNY, he joined a daily newspaper as copy boy, rose to sports writer, and then film critic. Later, he switched his writing and editing to magazines, directing the publishing activities of several different companies. He authored many sports biographies for young people until moving to London, England, several years ago. For a time he worked with Reuters, the British news agency, and was publishing director for the British branch of Warner Communications, Inc. Now married to an English woman, he is a freelance writer of paperback books, books for young people, and magazine articles.